Judith Cook was born in Manchester. A journalist for sixteen years, she was Arts Editor of the *Birmingham Post*, worked for *Labour Weekly* and was, and is, a regular contributor to the *Guardian*. She has worked in radio and was a reporter/researcher in television. She is the author of two previous books, *Director's Theatre* (1974) and *The National Theatre* (1976).

Apprentices of Freedom

Judith Cook

QUARTET BOOKS
LONDON   MELBOURNE   NEW YORK

For Martin

without whose encouragement and support
it would never have been completed

First published by Quartet Books Limited 1979
A member of the Namara Group
27 Goodge Street, London W1P 1FD

ISBN 0 7043 2186 6

Distributed in the U.S.A. by Horizon Press,
156 Fifth Avenue, New York, NY 10010

Photoset, printed and bound
in Great Britain by
REDWOOD BURN LIMITED
Trowbridge & Esher

Contents

Acknowledgements

I would like to acknowledge first the help and assistance of Nan Green Secretary of the International Brigade Association, including the use of the association's own taped material with which I supplemented my own. Thanks also to the Archive Department of the Imperial War Museum for their help and assistance spread over many months. I would like to express my gratitude, too, to Hywel Francis and the South Wales Miners' Library, the *New Statesman* and *Tribune* for helping me to contact volunteers to Spain and to Donald Ross of *Labour Weekly* for his encouragement. Encouragement came, too, from the late Maureen Prior, who died before the book was completed.

The quotations from W. H. Auden are from 'Spain 1937', which appears in *Collected Shorter Poems* (Faber) and from George Barker's 'Elegy for Spain' which appears in his *Collected Poems 1930-1955* (Faber). The other quotations are from members of the International Brigade.

Last, but not least, I must thank most sincerely all those men of the British Battalion of the XVth International Brigade who gave up so much of their time to help with this project. I can only say that I have tried to do them justice. Some of the veterans, including Albert Cole and Bill Feeley, died before publication.

Foreword
Jack Jones

'Why did people go to fight in Spain?' The answer is not an easy one, but some part of the reply is to be found in this book.

The awful realization that black fascism was on the march right across Europe created a strong desire to act. The march had started with Mussolini and had gained terrible momentum with Hitler and was being carried forward under Franco. For most young people there was a feeling of frustration, but some determined to do anything that seemed possible, even if it meant death, to try to stop the spread of fascism.

Unfortunately, too few people realized in Britain that democracy was at stake in Spain. A legitimate, democratically elected, government was under attack from an insurrection of military officers, and for some, anyway, that knowledge led to joining the majority of the Spanish people in resisting the revolt.

Here at least is something of the story of the brave people who left home and family to fight for an ideal. It's a story of courage and determination against enormous odds, and incredible difficulties.

Spain attracted my attention as a trade unionist. Before going to the Civil War I had already established links with the UGT through contacts with Spanish seamen in my work in the docks. This contact led not just to my going to Spain, but I was able to link up with the Spanish trade unions before and during my participation in the International Brigade. My association with the Spanish trade unions continued during the dark years of Franco's dictatorship and no one can be more proud than I am at the resurgence of the Spanish trade-union movement which is now taking place.

A new spirit is emerging which is inspiring the movement of democracy and the growth of free trade unionism in Spain. There is deep understanding that the shedding of blood and the sacrifices of the Civil War cannot be repeated, the terrible past calls out to the future, 'Never again!'

That message is bringing a deep response from the Spanish people. We, their friends here in Britain, must do all we can to help them in building their democracy and ensuring their freedom.

It is a somewhat different task from that undertaken by 'the soldiers of the Republic', but it represents a fundamental obligation for those who care for freedom and peace in the world.

This book will help to commemorate the story of those who felt that international solidarity required something more than reading about it at home. So many who took up the challenge failed to return – these pages provide a salute to their memory.

October 1978

Introduction

The Spanish Civil War became the focus of the fight against
·fascism in the 1930s. Of those who went and fought for the
Republic, some saw it as a crusade, others as a logical con-
tinuation of the workers' struggle. For the Germans and
Italians it was a useful rehearsal for the Second World War.
Yet it is not remembered as a war involving the working
class. It remains an intellectuals' war, seen through the eyes
of its distinguished participants, such as Julian Bell, John
Cornford, Philip Toynbee, George Orwell and Esmond
Romilly. It is *For Whom the Bell Tolls* and *Homage to Cata-
lonia*.

Yet 95 per cent of the Britons who fought in Spain came
from working-class backgrounds, from the shipyards,
mines and the hunger marches. Few had ever been abroad
before and most of them had to leave their families behind
them in great hardship. On their return, they did not sit
down and write of their experiences, yet they *were* the
British Battalion of the XVth International Brigade.

Less than 200 men survive from those who went to Spain.
This is the story of some of them, told in their own words.
Forty years have not dimmed the memories of those whose
feelings are summed up by Sam Wild, last commander of
the British Battalion: 'I've had experiences of all kinds, but
the happiest days of my life were spent in Spain. For the first
time I recognized the dignity, the goodness and the bravery
of ordinary people.'

With the re-emergence in recent years of a fascist movement in this country, it is as well to remember what happened last time.

1 The Volunteers

'Freedom is infectious. So we went to Spain so we could defeat Hitler. Those who went to fight in Spain were the apprentices of freedom who became freedom's craftsmen' – Bob Cooney, International Brigader from Aberdeen

Few events of this century have produced the emotional impact of the Spanish Civil War. For some it was, quite simply, a crusade. Others saw it as a dress rehearsal for what was to come later in 1939. The British government followed a policy of non-intervention and bitterly divided the nation. Those in this country who supported the Republic and remained politically active throughout their lives say that no other single issue has produced such a response from ordinary people.

It has, however, been considered very much an intellectuals' and writers' war. When one thinks of British participation it is in the terms of Esmond Romilly, George Orwell, Phillip Toynbee, Laurie Lee walking out one morning, poems from W. H. Auden, Stephen Spender and George Barker, all typified by the Byronic figure of the young poet John Cornford – a white bandage around his head – dying the day after his twenty-first birthday, having written of that quiet section of a quiet front.

Yet 95 per cent of those Britons who fought in Spain for the Republic, in fact came from a solid, working-class background. As the last commander of the British Battalion, Sam Wild, says: 'We all know about the artists and intellectuals. Laurie Lee was already there, Ralph and Winifred

Bates were bumming round Spain if I can use the expression. People like John Cornford and Esmond Romilly knew how to travel, how to get a passport, what to do. It took longer for us working men to organize ourselves but we went within a very short time.'

Figures differ, as we shall see, as to how many men went from Britain, but it was well over 2,000. There is no disagreement over the fact that a quarter of these were to die and well over 1,000 of the remainder were to be badly injured.

They came from all over the British Isles, but there were four main areas from which they came in strength: the valleys of the mining areas of South Wales, the Clydeside, Manchester and London.

When you look into their backgrounds before they went it is easy to see why this was. Almost all of them had, because of that background, been politically active before going to Spain. They had fought Mosley's blackshirts or had been active in the Unemployed Workers' Movement. Between two thirds and three quarters of them were communists, some were members of the ILP or Labour Party, others had no special political affiliation other than being vaguely left.

Most of them had left school very early to go into heavy manual labour – like shipbuilding or mining – and all too many had later found themselves victims of the Depression, drawing the dole or joining the hunger marches. But what is very striking in this day of packaged television politics and easy images, is how politically educated they were.

Aware of the advantages denied them of further education, they went to Workers' Education Association lectures, to the Young Communist League, to political meetings of all kinds and to their public libraries. They slogged their way through books on Marx and Engels, they read Tom Paine, and when they argued they knew what they were talking about.

They took to the streets in the anti-fascist activities of the 1930s, and it is interesting to see that what exercises us so much now – how to avoid violence in the streets between left and right – worried them not at all. Many of the Spanish volunteers talk with enthusiasm of the fights they had with 'Mosley's bloody fascists'. They tell you how they learned to bring mounted policemen down off their horses, how they learned tricks to give themselves an advantage when it came to a fight. Two ex-Clydeside workers told me with relish of wrenching heavy metal litter bins off lamp posts in Glasgow to go out and beat Mosley's men over the head with them. In Manchester, thanks largely to the organization of people like Sam Wild, Mosley hardly dared march at all.

They were not just young political hotheads. George Aitken, who became the International Brigade's political commissar, was already an established political figure and was forty-two years old.

As Hywel Francis of the South Wales Miners' Library says in his paper, 'Welsh Miners and the Spanish Civil War', 'they were neither youthful idealists or adventure-seeking bachelors. Their average age was over thirty and 18 per cent were married.' He also points out that 25 per cent of those who volunteered from Wales were trade-union officials.

The characteristics he points out as being strong in the areas from which the Welsh volunteers came, applied nationwide. They came from where there was a high level of unemployment and from the areas which tended to encourage a two-class structure and where the capitalist class was easily recognizable.

How they got to Spain will form a chapter on its own and, once the policy of non-intervention was strictly applied and the Franco-Spanish border closed, just getting there at all required enormous tenacity. As we shall see, people who had never gone in for more than a Sunday ramble, climbed the Pyrenees, and those who knew nothing of the sea risked stowing away.

The history of the Republic throughout the civil war is marred by interminable in-fighting, quarrels and wild swings of policy. The communists of the Popular Front were at bitter odds with POUM (a revolutionary Marxist

3

party) and both turned and rent the various anarchist and syndicalist movements such as the CNT (the Anarcho-Syndicalist Trades Union). Then there was the PSOE, the Spanish Socialist Party. There were divisions within the parties making up the Comintern (the Communist International), even within the British Communist Party itself. The Spanish Civil War was a tragedy of the fragmented left.

But little of the internal squabbles and fights over policy seem to have affected the men of the British Battalion – only a few became directly involved. It was at the time – and remains now – a simple matter. The war in Spain was fought to stop fascism.

They also saw the war from a trench-eye viewpoint. They were the 'poor bloody infantry' and basic questions of facing an enemy under fire, getting enough to eat, sheer survival, took up most of their time without political shades of opinion coming into it. They marched when they were told to, fought when they had to and took time off when they could scrounge it to go off and sleep, eat and drink wine.

Along with a white-hot commitment to the anti-fascist cause, they took with them prosaic good sense and a sense of humour. They showed the most amazing courage, most of them going into battle with barely three weeks' training and never having handled a weapon in their lives. They knew nothing of warfare, and one soldier describes his first sound of bullets from the opposing side as sounding like the odd gentle hum of bees.

They watched their friends and comrades killed beside them, and learned to bury them and carry on. One man described seeing his first dead men: 'Everywhere men are lying. Men with a curious ruffled look, like a dead bird.'

Many were never to come back, few escaped unhurt. Some were wounded several times and others still nurse their obvious wounds now in the form of blinded eyes and lost limbs. Still more paid for their involvement with years of ill-health following bullet wounds in the lungs or stomach.

Well over a hundred were taken prisoner and suffered very great hardship. It is remarkable to think of those steelworkers and miners ending up in concentration camps – before they had really been heard of here – and suffering interrogation from the Gestapo and coming out of the experience whole, sane and not having broken when they had had no training or preparation for anything of the kind. One man was shot in prison and others on the field, as examples to the rest.

Afterwards they returned to their homes and families and some went on to fight in 1939–45 in the Second World War.

The International Brigaders from Germany and Italy were prime targets after leaving Spain, and almost all of them vanished during the Second World War. Many of those from Easten Europe unhappily followed suit, although the position was somewhat different in Yugoslavia as Tito himself had been involved.

The Americans of the Abraham Lincoln Battalion were always suspect in the United States and the survivors had a pitifully hard time during the worst excesses of the McCarthy era as they were still considered as 'subversives'. They were persecuted right through into the early 1960s.

The British certainly fared better than this. Hugh Thomas, in *The Spanish Civil War*, states that few of the Britons who fought in Spain achieved much eminence afterwards. He mentions only the Member of Parliament Bob Edwards, who fought with POUM; and, in passing, Will Paynter, who became general secretary of the National Union of Mineworkers.

To the onlooker this seems odd. Even putting aside all those who did extremely well at local level and became councillors, trade-union officials, mayors and leading figures in the Communist and Labour Parties, the general secretaryship of the NUM is no mean achievement for anybody. He also ignores Jack Jones, who became general secretary of the Transport and General Workers' Union and who has more recently, in 1978, been made a Companion of Honour. He would seem to have achieved no small position of power, and even his most bitter opponents, such as the *Daily Mail*, paid him a backhanded compliment in recent years when they referred to him as 'Emperor Jones' and 'the most powerful man in Britain'.

In the nature of things, those who fought in Spain are now elderly. But, in a curious way, time has dealt kindly with the survivors and many look younger than they are. However, they are gradually getting less and there are now under 200 survivors left of those Britons who went to Spain.

Over the years, the differences that divided them following their return from the Spanish Civil War have faded and they have mellowed. Those who remained in the Communist Party now have contact with those who did not, and all meet through the efforts of the International Brigade Association. A reunion held in this country in 1976 brought together survivors from all over the world.

The most striking thing they have in common is how they look back now on their time in Spain. Without exception it remains, for them, the highspot of their lives. Nothing since has been able to match it. They are unshaken in their belief that they were absolutely right to have gone.

It is remarkable that a small band of untrained, badly armed men could produce such a roll of battle honours: Madrid, Jarama, Brunete, Teruel, Belchite, Gandesa and the Ebro.

It was obviously not possible to put every survivor's story into this book. What follows are the reminiscences and experiences of a representative number whose story is followed from their political activities in this country in the 1930s, through their time in Spain, until their return home. There are also material and anecdotes from other veterans whose stories do not appear in full, and those who are not mentioned by name will it is hoped feel that they have not gone unrecorded. It is an attempt to show the other side of that 'intellectuals' war' and to record it before it is too late.

It was a moving experience and a rare privilege to listen to the men of the British Battalion of the XVth International Brigade. There has been nothing like it since and the overwhelming advance of military technology will ensure there is nothing like it again. It was almost the last time, at least in Europe, that men thought they could go out on the streets and fight tanks with their bare hands and win. Their cry of *No pasarán*, 'They shall not pass', comes down to us this day.

2   The War in Outline

It would be impossible in a short space to detail the history of the Spanish Civil War. There is plenty of material available on its origins, its political and economic implications and its long-term effects. But it is necessary to give a brief outline so that the events described by the participants can be put into context.

It is also a confusing conflict to describe. At its most basic, no one source, either the historians or the museum archive material available, agrees even on the numbers of people involved, let alone how many were killed, wounded or taken prisoner. There are various reasons for this, including the fact that it was not an 'official' war in that no official bodies kept a careful note on how many fought and where. Again, both sides exaggerated the losses of the enemy and played down their own; and from the point of view of the foreign volunteers, they kept very quiet about their involvement both before and after going to Spain as they were not supposed to have been there at all.

When hostilities began on 17 July 1936, Spain had been a Republic for over five years. The Republic had been characterized by the inability of its leadership to agree on many issues. There were interminable internal quarrels, a growing threat from the right and the rising nationalist aspirations of the Basques and Catalans.

After a sporadic outburst of political assassinations, the Nationalist rebellion began in Morocco on 16 July followed by a number of risings in Spain on the 18th. The Nationalist forces were very shortly to come under the command of

General Franco.

As Hugh Thomas points out, the constitutional means of opposing the rising met with failure, and did so inevitably because many of the forces of law and order – the army and the Civil Guard – were with the rebels, who themselves claimed to represent law and order. 'The only force capable of resisting the rebels', he says, 'was that of the trade unions and left-wing parties. Yet for the government to use that force would mean that it accepted revolution.'

The early weeks of the war were marked by appalling violence on both sides. Atrocity stories abound, and even discounting those used for propaganda purposes – or the fact that the same stories appear attributed to both sides – there is no doubt that the slaughter of civilians was very terrible indeed.

For instance, in July in the working-class district of Triana in Seville, the Moorish troops assembled all the able-bodied men and bayoneted them to death after castrating them. As we will see later, the Moors became synonymous with excessive cruelty, and by the end of the war, by a supreme irony, men of the International Brigades found themselves in prison with those same Moors, the Nationalists having decided that their behaviour had become too extreme.

People were flogged, tortured and maimed to death, were burned and buried alive. It was a time, too, for settling private feuds and grudges. Most of those who vanished into unknown, unmarked graves were themselves unknown, but it was during this period that Spain lost its most remarkable writer: the poet Frederico García Lorca. Nobody has ever taken the responsibility for his death and nobody knows exactly where he died or where he is buried.

However, there seems to be general agreement that while the worst excesses of the Republicans mainly took place during the first two months of the war, the execution of Republican civilians by the Nationalists continued throughout its three-year span. It became an accepted part of the Nationalist administration, and they were taught by the masters of the genre. Germany sent officers of the Gestapo into Spain to advise and use interrogation techniques, and it is not sufficiently well known that Britons of the International Brigade suffered at their hands before the outbreak of the Second World War. It is impossible to know how many civilians died – a figure of 110,000 is an average – but it seems that more than half of them died between July and September 1936.

When the war began, Spain was roughly divided into two. The Nationalists held northern Spain – apart from the coastal strip around Santander, the Asturias and the Basque country – in a line roughly from midway along the Portuguese–Spanish border, bending round north of Madrid and Guadalajara, looping south again to Teruel and driving due north to midway along the Franco-Spanish frontier. They also held a small triangle in the south made up of the areas around Huelva, Seville and Cádiz. The Nationalist area was the poorer in natural resources but possessed stronger ones in the way of men, material and a well-trained army. The Republican area was commercially and industrially the stronger but was weakened by internal conflict.

Britain and France, throughout the conflict, followed their policy of non-intervention in the teeth of growing evidence that Germany and Italy were sending in large quantities of men and armaments. There were regular deliveries of arms by sea and air from Germany to Spain throughout the duration of the war, and it was the increasingly weighted imbalance of men and machinery which was to make Franco's victory more and more certain. For the purposes of this book, Franco's forces are referred to as the Nationalists and those of the government of the day as the Republicans.

Hostilities began in the summer of 1936 with the battles around Madrid. Franco and the Nationalists were never to achieve their ambition of taking the capital by force of arms. Madrid fell without a struggle right at the end of the war. But while fighting in central Spain, Franco also pushed hard in the north where the Republicans held two areas: those of the Asturias and the Basque country.

It was not a war of cool strategy nor was it recorded afterwards in the way of the First and Second World Wars. Battles had overtones of both conflicts. The battle of Jarama in early 1937 was followed by months of stalemate in the trenches reminiscent of the First World War, while the German and Italian troops and airmen used some of the later battles in Spain as rehearsals for the Second. But the Republican forces were always thinly stretched, and while they managed to hold Franco on the Jarama front, he finally succeeded in his conquest first of the Basque country and then of the Asturias.

On a number of occasions, at Brunete and on the Aragón, and finally on the last crossing of the Ebro, the Republicans launched diversionary offensives which were to be initially successful but would fail through lack of a coherent policy as well as a lack of men and necessary equipment.

But whatever the result of each individual battle, the maps of the war show the relentless drive of the Nationalists towards the sea to cut the Republic in two. In the winter of 1937–8, the Republicans tried desperately to stop this from happening. Their initial attack in the Aragón succeeded in delaying the Nationalist advance, but by April 1938 the Aragón front had collapsed and the Nationalists had succeeded in their objective and reached the Mediterranean at Vinarez.

In July 1938, the Republican war council decided that unless there was a further diversionary attack elsewhere, Valencia would fall, and launched their last offensive of the war. It was decided to cross the Ebro some seventy miles from the sea. The crossing began on the night of 25 July, and in spite of the months of massive setbacks it looked very hopeful. It even shook the Nationalists; it was ruthless, effective and a surprise. To the Republicans, it seemed as if a miracle still might happen, but Franco was determined to push them back at whatever cost, and by 2 August the advance was contained.

The two armies slogged it out through the month of August, with the Republicans performing amazing feats of repair work on the Ebro bridges under constant bombardment. In September 1938 events outside Spain overtook everybody, and this is not the time or place to go into the well-known results of the Munich conference, Chamberlain's 'peace in our time' and Hitler's invasion of Czechoslovakia.

As it is the experience of the British volunteers which follows, it is obvious that the sequence of the war is seen in the order in which it affected them and the British Battalion and International Brigades were not involved on all the fronts.

The Germans and Italians had reacted to the situation in Spain swiftly, and as soon as hostilities began in the summer of 1936 they began sending bombers and the first contingent of trained German troops left for Spain. Heinkel and Junker aircraft followed.

The earliest volunteers from Britain, who included the poet John Cornford, arrived well before the formation of either the British Battalion or the XVth Brigade of which it was to become part. They fought in the battles in and around Madrid in the summer of 1936 and at Lopera and Las Rozas at Christmas 1936 and in the New Year of 1937.

It was towards the end of this period that the formation of the International Brigades took place, undertaken by the Comintern (the Communist International). Each European communist party was asked to supply volunteers, but by no means were all those who volunteered for Spain communists. Among those who processed the volunteers and even, it is said, later fought in Spain was Josip Broz, now known as Marshal Tito, although he has always denied his participation. Many British volunteers are convinced they saw him there, including Maurice Levine and Fred Copeman, whose fortunes we follow in this book.

The central office of the Brigades was in Paris, and here the volunteers were vetted. The first contingent of 500 of mixed nationalities left for Spain towards the end of October and eventually went to what was to become the headquarters of the Brigades at Albacete.

Hugh Thomas puts the number of foreigners who fought for the Republic at about 40,000, 35,000 of whom fought with the Brigades. The largest group came from France, the rest from Britain, Austria, Germany, Poland, Scandinavia, Yugoslavia, Hungary, Czechoslovakia, Canada and the United States. There were approximately 2,000 Britons. Neil Wood, in *Communism and British Intellectuals*, says there were 2,762 British volunteers, of whom 1,762 were wounded and 543 killed, but no other source is so precise. The first sizeable group, 145 of them, formed the No. 1 Company which was attached to the mainly French XIVth Brigade.

It was on the Jarama, in the early days of February 1937, that the British Battalion, as a separate entity and part of the newly formed XVth Brigade, saw action for the first time. The central figure in its formation was the legendary George Nathan, who became famous in Spain not only for his military acumen but for his bravery and pristine appearance whatever the conditions. The first political commissar was David Springhall, soon to be replaced by George Aitken.

To the outsider it looks as if, throughout their time in Spain, the British Battalion bore the brunt of any offensive in which they were engaged. Time and again they were sent out on a limb, with raw recruits being flung into action with little or no training. It was typical that during the battle of Jarama it was the British who defended the so-called 'suicide hill' for more than seven hours against artillery and machine guns and armed only with nineteenth-century rifles.

Looked at now, forty years on, it seems unlikely that the Republic could have won, having to cope with the lack of armaments and men caused by the non-intervention policy, and riven by internal conflicts. Throughout the war there existed the old, old problem of a unified right fighting a fragmented left.

After Jarama, the next major battle in which the British took part was at Brunete. The XVth Brigade, used as a shock force, suffered terrible losses. So heavy were they that some battalions had to be merged and virtually all those in positions of command in the British Battalion were either killed or wounded. Nathan was to die at Brunete. The strength of the British Battalion, which had reached 600 in January 1937, was reduced to 80 men. At Brunete, the German Condor Legion, with its Messerschmitt fighters, appeared in battle for the first time to all-too-great effect.

Brunete showed with awful clarity the disparity between the sides. Figures again differ, but Édouard de Blaye says that, by the end of 1937, the Republic could at most put into the field 450,000 men, including the International Brigades, while Franco's forces numbered over 650,000, including crack German and Italian troops. They also had superiority in the air.

The British took part in the diversionary Aragón offensive in the early part of 1938 and in the bitter retreat which followed in the late spring. Their final participation was in the last great battles of the Ebro. The remnants of the XVth Brigade fought desperately hard in a number of engagements, and again the British Battalion found themselves fighting on an isolated hill, this time Hill 481. On the Jarama it had been 'suicide hill', on the Ebro it was Hill 481. The result was the same. The losses were very heavy indeed.

What became a war of attrition on the Ebro left the Republicans exhausted in every way. They lost tens of thousands of men. On 22 September, the XVth International Brigade and the British Battalion went into action for the last time, resulting in the death of many Britons on the last day they were involved.

Before the Ebro campaign was over, the International Brigades had been withdrawn. The Republican premier, Juan Negrín, had suggested it should be done under the auspices of the League of Nations. This extremely controversial decision was taken in a vain hope that the Germans and Italians would also withdraw their troops, and that even at this late stage the Republic could hold out. It was a futile move.

On 15 November the International Brigades gathered together for the last time at a parade in Barcelona and heard Negrín himself and La Pasionaria, the great communist heroine of the war, bid them farewell. 'You can go proudly,' Pasionaria told them. 'You are history. You are legend.'

After the withdrawal of the International Brigades, Franco mounted a massive offensive. In January 1939 Barcelona finally fell without resistance. By February the British government had recognized the Franco régime as the 'official Government of Spain'. Nobody could have guessed then that, despite the Second World War, which was to defeat Hitler and Mussolini and was supposed to end fascism in Europe, the régime in Spain was destined to last for a further forty years.

As Hugh Thomas says: 'The Spanish Civil War exceeded in ferocity most wars between nations ... The manner in which the military rebellion was carried out and in which the Republican Government replied to it in the first hours, caused a breakdown in restraint such as had not been seen in Europe since the Thirty Years War.'

It has taken recent history, in Vietnam, to show that it is possible to take on a superior military technology, coupled with trained foreign troops, and win. But maybe the difference lies in the fact that the war in Vietnam was basically a truly nationalist conflict and this in itself ensured that unity of the left which, tragically, was never achieved during the course of the war in Spain.

3 Protesters in the 'Thirties (1)

The Clydeside shipyard workers' leader Jimmy Reid told a story at the Fortieth Birthday Rally of *Tribune* in 1977. A do-gooding, middle-class lady came to the Clydeside in the early 1930s and was telling a group of wives of unemployed workers how to make a nourishing soup out of fish-heads and fish-bones. Jimmy's mother watched with interest. 'Aye,' she said at the end, 'very interesting. And who gets the rest of the fish?'

*

Whoever was getting the rest of the fish in the early 1930s, it was not the average working-class worker, wherever he lived.

Of the volunteers for Spain, the Scots and the Welsh shared much in common. They came from the areas of heavy industry – mines, shipyards, steelworks – with a strong sense of individualism and national identity. They were also hit very heavily indeed by the years of depression and unemployment, and, as we have seen in our own day, it is in these conditions that fascism thrives. Also, because of the closeness of the communities, the Scots and Welsh documented their activities among themselves and on their return kept in touch more easily.

From these two areas come, therefore, a number of those whose fortunes will be followed through the years of the war: Sid Quinn, Bob Cooney, Garry McCartney, Edward Brown, William Kelly, Joseph Hughes and George Drever from Scotland and Will Paynter from Wales.

Soaring unemployment and cuts in wages were felt all over Britain, but nowhere worse than on Clydeside. From this background of deprivation, poverty and strong conviction came the Scots who went to Spain. Almost all of them had a solid history of protest behind them before they set off. Figures compiled recently by Garry McCartney, Scottish secretary of the International Brigade Association, show that some 467 Scotsmen went to Spain. Of these, 134 were killed, 30 taken prisoner and 342 returned, some very badly wounded. They came from all over Scotland, but especially from Glasgow and the Clydeside and from Aberdeen.

Sid Quinn was born in Lisburn, County Antrim, the thirteenth child out of a family of fourteen, to Roman Catholic parents. His father went to Glasgow in search of work as a plasterer. The mother died, leaving ten orphans. 'I was a boy in the real barefoot days,' he says. 'My young brother died of galloping TB in 1922 – in fact, half my family were wiped out with the same disease.'

He became politically active through the interest of his brother, and gravitated naturally towards the Communist Party. 'If you had a modicum of intelligence you knew you were being conned – the working class had been conned for years.'

He left school at fourteen, worked as a grocer's boy and remained with the grocer until he became unemployed at the age of twenty in 1931, when he went on his first hunger march to London.

He was much influenced by Harry McShane and the late Peter Kerrigan ('Big Pete'). Unable to find work he joined the army. 'I had no ulterior motive for joining the army. I was young, there were no prospects, it's as simple as that. I didn't intend to be seditious or anything. I was never so hardcore a revolutionary that I thought I could alter the world by my own unaided efforts.'

He continued reading his communist literature and going to meetings when he could, and during Mussolini's invasion

17

of Abyssinia he was shipped out to Aden. 'I'd held fast to my beliefs – I've never seen cause to change them to this day – and I remember when it was proposed calling troops in to drive during some dispute that I objected. Anyway, I got measles in Aden and was sent home, whether for political or medical reasons I've never been sure, but I think it was for political reasons. By 1936 I was back on the dole and hunger marching again. I was also involved in the anti-Mosley protests. I never did much speaking though or things like that, I was never very enthusiastic about meetings.'

Sid did not seek out violence, but others lapped it up. One veteran from Spain, who came from the Gorbals, says: 'I had the privilege of assisting Sir Oswald Mosley to the ground with a piece of lead piping . . .' Bob Cooney from Aberdeen would no doubt have approved as he was always in the thick of it. He typifies another kind of volunteer.

His first political activity was with the No More War Movement, and his education was an avid reading of everything political he could lay his hands on in the public library. He spent hours at the Links and Castlegate in Aberdeen where the big open-air political meetings were held. He worked in an office, but got the sack after having taken a Sunday off to attend a political meeting.

'I used to go to the Links, it was a kind of Open University. There were speakers from the CP, Anti-Parliamentary Movement, Independent Labour Party [ILP], Reconstruction League, everybody. Anyway, by the early 'thirties I'd joined the great heap of the unemployed.'

He first joined the ILP Guild of Youth, and then moved to the Communist Party as he felt the ILP did not take enough of a stand against the growing fascist movement in the country. 'One reason for my concern was that we had one of the leaders of the British Union of Fascists in Aberdeen – he'd learned his fascism in South Africa and he'd learned it well. We fought those buggers for two years or more and built up tremendous opposition.

'We developed a way of hunting them out. They had a van and a car in the early part of 1935, and every tram and bus

18

conductor was our ally. They'd tell us where they were going. The BUF [British Union of Fascists] daren't advertise their meetings any more, they had them on a hit-and-run basis. We'd teams of youngsters on cycles tracking them down. They'd always go to working-class streets and sometimes we'd be too late because the women had already dealt with them. Then we'd chase them for thirty or forty miles to Peterhead and Fraserburgh.

'We had a supporter in Peterhead, an old, sick chap called Tony Stevens. Once when the BUF arrived there he went and rang the school bell and shouted to the kiddies – the Spanish War had just begun – "These are the black-shirted bastards who murder kiddies in Spain. Spit on them, kids!" And they did, they spat on them.'

He marched, demonstrated, fought – 'I felt we had to smash them off the streets' – appearing so regularly in court 'they began to think I was breaking into prison I was there so often. Kerrigan used to get very annoyed. He was a stern-looking chap in those days, a great disciplinarian. He was much senior to me in the party, and whenever he came to Aberdeen I wanted to hide. I was terrified of him. He'd always find something you hadn't done. In fact, I got into so much trouble that when the time came to go to Spain I had problems. They thought I was too temperamental and would be a heavy risk.'

Disillusion with the Labour Party and ILP drove many into the Communist Party. Edward Brown of Glasgow describes the Labour Party as 'selling out' over unemployment and the rise of fascism, William Kelly was generally dissatisfied. Garry McCartney joined the Young Communist League in Glasgow in 1932, 'mostly as the result of my colleagues' most eloquent style and their sincere advocacy of the things that mattered in those days – as indeed they do today. They looked for a change in society.

'Glasgow was the centre of the industrial working class, you couldn't be anything else if you worked there. It was really politically motivated, this city of ours, and the title it had for many years of the "Red City" was accurate and very noticeable in those days. It may have been because of the most deprived times that the aftermath of the First World War brought about. We'd such tremendous unemployment and poverty. In the agonies of the hungry 'thirties, when three million were unemployed in Britain, again the west of Scotland suffered badly as it does today. So it was the natural thing for most young people, and certainly mature men who had come through the war, to have real socialist leanings, and most of that rubbed off on me. We were a fertile ground.

'At any time there'd be political groups meeting on street corners. You didn't have the money to rent halls so the streets were the open forums of the day and politics was a very, very much spoken word. So when the Spanish War broke out we were already aware that we were living in a world, or part of it anyway, of fascism.

'It was the natural way of things that young people felt that rather than just talk about being anti-fascist, the opportunity had afforded itself to do something concrete. Hence the reason why, size for size, Glasgow gave the most volunteers to the Republic of almost any city, I think, in Europe.'

The political background of those who went from Wales was not dissimilar, although it tended towards efforts against unemployment rather than anti-fascism. Hywel Francis of the South Wales Miners' Library puts the figure of those who went to Spain at 170. The largest single area from which they came was that of the mining valleys of the Rhondda, Aberdare and Merthyr. Among them, 104 were communists, the rest Labour or ILP, and there was one Liberal. Some twenty-five had been arrested for political activity, twenty-five had marched on hunger marches and thirty-five were trade-union officials.

Their average age was over thirty, and 18 per cent were married.

This [says Hywel Francis in 'Welsh Miners and the Spanish Civil War'] could be seen in its social context. All the Welsh miners who were married had also been unemployed for long periods. Unemployment had probably alienated some from their communities and from their families, while Spain could easily be seen as an escape to adventure from boredom, frustration and a meaningless existence. On the other hand, 38 per cent of the Welsh unemployed miners who had volunteered had been victimized for their trade-union activities.

Typical of these was Will Paynter, who later became general secretary of the Nation Union of Mineworkers. 'The first miners' lockout stimulated my interest in what was going on and why, though I only joined the CP in 1929. I was employed in the Cymmer Colliery at Porth in the Rhondda. I'd been there since 1918, a collier working on the coal face. We had the 1926 General Strike and the lockout which was connected with it and which lasted nine days. In a way, the General Strike had less significance in the Rhondda as it is such a one-industry area that a strike in the mines is effectually a General Strike.' He went to meetings, and there was a very good library attached to the colliery, which 'had very good socialist books and I gravitated towards Marxism after reading Marx, Engels and so on – they influenced my outlook. I had some difficulty about joining the CP because of my domestic situation which was not uncommon in South Wales.

'My mother was very religious, very respectable. I'd been an almost compulsory chapelgoer even when I'd taken to reading communist papers. It became in the end almost a domestic crisis.'

He took part in the election campaign for the local Communist Party candidate, Arthur Horner, in 1928, and became deeply involved in politics. His political activity took up larger and larger amounts of time and, like his Scottish comrades, he began getting arrested.

'One of the first big involvements over the Spanish War came in July 1936 when I was acting organizer for the South Wales Communist Party. Harry Pollitt phoned down to say that Baldwin had gone down to take a holiday in Wales as

Parliament was in recess. He was staying in Mongomery-shire with a coal owner. The party was developing a campaign for the recall of Parliament because of the Spanish War and I was requested to take as substantial a deputation as I could to discuss the situation, confront Baldwin and demand the recall of Parliament to do something on the matter under its obligations to the League of Nations.

'We got together a delegation from miners' lodges, councils, trades councils and so on, and with two borrowed cars drove up from mid-Wales. We got to Newtown, close to the estate, and in the afternoon marched to the house. It was a beautiful estate with a long drive and flowers everywhere, and then we came to a turnoff and saw this beautiful mansion. We knocked on the door and a little Welsh maid came out and we asked to see Mr Baldwin. She said he wasn't in, we said we didn't believe her and she burst into tears and we were lost . . . So I left a note saying we'd be calling back the following day.

'We went back the following day after trying to hold a couple of meetings to arouse the people of Newtown – and it's a hell of a job arousing the people of Newtown – but when we got there, to the little turnoff, a mass of plain-clothes policemen or special-branch men or something came out from behind the bushes and trees with sticks and drove us off. We couldn't reach the house. We tried to take photographs but it was difficult. We never did see Baldwin, but our main idea was to get publicity for the recall of Parliament. This failed – there was very little. I think there was government pressure on newspapers not to tell of the situation.'

4 Protesters in the 'Thirties (2)

Those who volunteered from England did not, apart from the Manchester contingent, come from anything like such tightly-knit communities as the Scots and Welsh. They came from the big cities and the small towns, often the only volunteer from that particular area, and because of this their experiences tended to be more diverse. The handful of Irish volunteers were individuals acting very much on their own.

Among our men, England provided Sam Wild, destined to be the British Battalion's commander, Joe Norman, Maurice Levine, Walter Greenhalgh, Bill Feeley, the buccaneering Charles Morgan, Albert Cole, Fred Copeman (also a battalion commander) and the much-respected George Aitken. From Ireland came one of the war's true freelances, Bob Doyle.

Because they were so scattered, therefore, there are no statistics of the make-up of the English volunteers, nor is it possible to know exactly how many there were of them. On their return some, especially in Manchester and London, did keep in touch. Others drifted away altogether, and their neighbours have no knowledge of their involvement in what all the men refer to as 'the Spanish War'.

Sam Wild was born in Ardwick in 1908, and his father was a fitter. 'I lived in a tough environment and had an unstable education. I went to fourteen schools . . . then I left at the age of fourteen.' He remembers being impressed by the Irish Rebellion of 1916, at the age of eight, and at the next General Election mobilized groups of kids to work for the local Labour candidate. He worked first for a printer, who went bankrupt, then did jobbing bricklaying, odd jobs and finally, with no work in sight, joined the navy when he was fifteen and a half.

'At this time my father was out of work, my brother in an orphanage and my sister in service. I joined the navy because it was a way to a meal ticket. I had no enthusiasm for life at sea. Life on a boys' training ship, HMS *Colossus*, was rigorous and strict, the food monotonous but at least regular.' And he became bantamweight boxing champion of his ship. It was while cruising in the Mediterranean on the *Resolution* 'that I became a potential rebel. I saw many things wrong and it made me anti-discipline and got me in frequent trouble. It could have been much more serious had I not been a good all-round sportsman.'

Trips round the British Empire – showing the Flag – showed him 'the appalling poverty of the people and the attitude of the British towards them. In 1931 the Invergordon Mutiny broke out and its impact on the rest of the navy was considerable.'

Finally Sam was sent to South Africa, and what he saw there made him 'unable to tolerate the navy and its outdated attitudes so I deserted'. He was arrested by the military police, tried for desertion and finally discharged – ineligible for unemployment benefit. He was then, he says, lucky to get a job as a boilerman in a cinema.

Work for the National Unemployed Workers' Movement followed and the now-familiar pattern of marches and anti-Mosley activity. This was so effective that Manchester eventually became a place where Mosley just did not go.

Maurice Levine from Manchester also learned his socialism through foreign travel. He had almost given the country up, and emigrated to Australia in 1928, thinking it would be a land of opportunity. He tramped the countryside looking for work, occasionally being picked up by the police as a vagrant, 'and there the vague socialist ideas I had in my youth became clarified. I saw starvation wages while peaches and apricots lay ankle-deep in the orchards of Northern Victoria because it just didn't pay the farmers to pick the fruit.

'I ranged the country looking for work for weeks and weeks and was eventually jailed for seven days in Adelaide after being caught as a stowaway on a ship from Melbourne. So I went back to England in 1931 and joined the CP.

'I became radicalized. In the succeeding years you had the growth and emergence of the Mosley fascists. Being politically conscious and having participated in a couple of hunger marches, I felt fascism was hell-bent on war.'

Joe Norman, still active in the Labour Party, was then in the Communist Party. He was a lad of diverse activity, editing a factory newspaper, joining the RNVR, and he was yet another International Brigade amateur boxing champion – he was a welterweight boxer. He became North of England Welterweight Champion for the navy and through this toured Europe, including the Soviet Union, as a member of the British Workers' Sports Federation Boxing Team.

'My first real experience of political activity, however, was the mass trespass on Kinderscout in Derbyshire which eventually led to the designation of the area as a National Park. Dozens of those who fought the police and landowners on that mass trespass were later to fight and die in Spain – men like Clem Beckett and George Brown. Some received up to six months hard labour for that trespass.' When the Spanish Civil War broke out, he was chairman of the local branch of the NUWM.

Walter Greenhalgh, whose time in Spain was largely to be spent as a courier, had a similar Manchester training in radical protest, but others, such as Charles Morgan and Bill Feeley (who came from St Helens), admit they had no particular political experience before Spain.

Charles Morgan, who must have been the buccaneer of the Battalion, is still fighting the class war, as he calls it, now. In the light of his personality it does not seem surprising that he went to Spain in the same batch as Errol Flynn ('Nice enough chap, can't think why they made all that fuss about the bugger's sex life . . .'). 'I wasn't involved in the class struggle before Spain. I had ideas that things were not right and hung on the fringe of the Unemployed Workers' Movement.

'That was mostly because I was unemployed and living on 15s. 3d. a week. I was single and it was companionship, and you could go to a dance and get a cup of tea for 3d.' He got fed up with this and went off and joined the Foreign Legion for three years where he found they did not encourage either individualism or socialism. 'But I was politically dumb. I was a nitwit. I don't make any claims that I went out as a crusader, it would be hypocrisy.'

Bill Feeley said that 'with all the unemployment we were looking for a way out. They used to come and recruit for the colonies, and some lads jumped at it, but when they got out there they found themselves just as exploited.'

Of the rest of our little group from the north, Albert Cole was one of a small contingent from Liverpool. His pre-war experiences were similar to many other volunteers, but his time in Spain was very different as he was one of the handful of Britons who fought with the Spanish Republican navy before joining the International Brigades later in the war.

Along from London came another sailor, Fred Copeman. He was on HMS *Resolution* at the time of the Invergordon Mutiny in which he took an active part, and he was yet another amateur boxing champion. After his participation in the mutiny, however, the navy felt they could manage without his prowess as a boxer and he left precipitately. 'No, it wasn't because I was a communist. I didn't join the party until I was nearly dying in Spain and Harry Pollitt came to see me and said it would be a bloody tragedy if I died without joining. I was sacked from many jobs, "Get that bloody Red out," they'd say, and I went to prison five times for the NUWM, but I never joined the CP.'

Like the rest he went on hunger marches and demonstrations. 'I was useful. I'd been taught how to handle horses in Norfolk as a young lad and I didn't get frightened when they charged us. This farmer taught me how to get one finger up its nostril and just grab. I'd a few battles that way. I remember sitting on the chest of the Commissioner of

Police for the City of London, Turnbull. He wanted to divert our hunger march around King's Cross, and I said, "Oh, no, mate, we're going straight on down the Strand," and up he came riding on his big white horse.

'The next thing off he came and I was sitting on his fanny on the floor. Years and years later I met him at a banquet in the City and he said, "Haven't I seen you somewhere before?" and I said, "You certainly did, mate, but from a different bloody angle . . ."

'I fought the fascists before I knew much about politics at all because they were just arrogant, bloody bastards looking for a fight. Gerald Gardiner, who became Labour Lord Chancellor, defended me a couple of times.'

Bob Doyle had an even more delicate political background. He was one of the small but noticeable Irish contingent of whom the best known was Kit Conroy. Bob was born in Dublin, 'and I actually managed to get a job when I was thirteen, the only one of my large family in work. But when that job finished I could find nothing so I went to Liverpool to see if I could do any better.

'I found nothing and soon got picked up by the police and was returned home. It was the time of the Right to Work marches and people were just learning about fascism. When I got back to Ireland I was determined to do something and ended by joining the Republican movement. I was very much influenced by Kit Conroy, later killed in Spain.

'I joined the 1st Battalion of the IRA until it split. The new IRA, as it was called, attracted me more as it had a broader base and it was more left wing. The Communist Party did not get started in Ireland, you see, until 1934. Anyway, I remember going along to see Sean Murray of the new IRA and proudly taking a revolver. I told him it was necessary to carry arms. He gave me an enormous and severe lecture and said that when the time came for people to use arms they would be provided and the people trained, but now was not the time. The progressives of the IRA then formed themselves into the IRA Congress and I joined that.

It participated in strikes, lockouts, evictions, all kinds of activities, rent strikes ... It had more appeal than the old IRA as it wasn't so insular and nationalistic.'

Last but not least is George Aitken, who although a radical and independent Scot achieved such eminence in the Communist Party – which he was to leave immediately after the Spanish War – that he was already a national and indeed international figure. He was a founder member of the Communist Party in Britain.

Aitken was one of the few members of the British Battalion to have previous military experience. He had served in the Black Watch in the First World War and been wounded and discharged as 'no longer physically fit'.

He became an efficient and active member of the Communist Party on returning from the war, drawn towards socialism by the massacre he had seen in the trenches and the treatment meted out to the men when they returned to a land which was supposed to be fit for heroes. He visited the Soviet Union in the 1920s and met the leaders of the Russian Revolution. He was the first manager of the *Daily Worker*, now the *Morning Star*, and although he came from the same hard background as the others, he was the only one who was a truly professional political activist before Spain. His abilities were to make him first commissar of the British Battalion, and then commissar to the XVth International Brigade.

Because of the very high number of wounded, hardly any of the remaining survivors of the British Battalion saw the Spanish War through from its beginning to when the International Brigades were withdrawn. But between them they can provide a continuing story of the war which starts with the efforts they made to get there.

5   Journey into War

'They clung like burrs to the long expresses that lurch
Through the unjust lands, through the night, through the
  alpine tunnel.
They floated over the oceans;
They walked the passes: they came to present their lives.'
  — W. H. Auden, 'Spain 1937'

For many volunteers the effort of going abroad at all was a problem. Few had even crossed the Channel, the majority had no passports and no experience of getting one or of how to set about foreign travel. 'We didn't even know how to get to London,' joked one of the Glasgow veterans. 'I did,' replied Sid Quinn. 'I knew every bloody foot of the way. I'd walked it twice on hunger marches . . .'

Most of those volunteering for Spain got into the country in one of two ways. In the early days the border between France and Spain was still open so that did not present a problem. The recruit would take a special weekend excursion ticket to Paris, available because the Great Exhibition was on, and once there would register with the Communist Party who would look after him and then dispatch him across France and into Spain either by train or bus. The beauty of the Great Exhibition scheme was that visitors to it did not require passports.

However, as time went on, getting to Spain presented formidable problems. For those entering later there was still the special weekend ticket, but by this time the police were taking a much greater interest in those using it and potential soldiers had to take much more care. By the time the main flood of volunteers left this country the way into Spain lay by the second route. This consisted of an undercover journey across France to the Spanish border and then entry on foot, by night, along smuggling routes which were to be used later in the Second World War. It was hazardous and difficult, especially as few men were equipped for climbing mountains, and those using the route spent much of their time dodging fascist patrols.

Again there were the few that used other methods, such as Bob Doyle, who stowed away and then jumped ship.

Among those who went into Spain more or less conventionally were Sid, Maurice Levine, Edward Brown, Phil Gillan, George Aitken, Walter Greenhalgh and Sam Wilde.

The early volunteers found problems even convincing the Communist Party in King Street to let them go. If they were not party members then they were regarded with suspicion; if they were, and were active, then it was felt they would be more useful at home.

Maurice Levine sums up the experiences of those early volunteers. He had tried to go straight away. Two friends from Manchester – Clem Beckett and Arnold Jeans – had already gone. Clem Beckett was a top-rank professional racing motor-cyclist and Arnold Jeans had been a private tutor to the Queen Mother's family in Russian and German. Both were to die. Maurice left Manchester with five other volunteers, the first organized party apart from Beckett and Jeans. Of the six Manchester lads who went with him, three died in the early battles of the war.

The first arrivals had their own problems with the processing authorities in Paris.

'On arriving,' said Maurice, 'we went straight away to an address somewhere in the Place de Combat and presented ourselves to a Spaniard who had a little office in a Maison de Syndicates. We had a little difficulty making ourselves understood, but he soon gathered that we were offering our services to fight in Spain for the Republic.

30

'On discovering we had no papers or credentials of any kind he had no interest in our mission. "No paper, no go," he said. We replied that we were all members of the Communist Party. "*Ça ne fait rien* – no paper, no go."

'We were at a loss to know what to do, and I suggested we inform the people next door of our plight. It was the office of the Metal Workers' Union. They were more accommodating and suggested they would find us a hotel and we should wait developments. In fact they delegated one of their staff to meet us each evening in Paris and keep us in touch. We pooled our francs and our total funds were quite low. It was croissants and coffee most of the time. One evening our guide took us to Les Halles, pointing out that certain cafés and bistros were frequently used by fascist supporters. As a special treat he ordered English tea. We did not like to mention that we had not had a proper meal for days.'

A week later their credentials arrived and they were accepted. 'We had to go to the Gare Austerlitz and find a certain pillar on the concourse where we would be met by someone who would give us rail tickets. We were told not to indulge in conversation with anyone and to be as unobtrusive as possible.' His party travelled by train to Perpignan and then crossed the Spanish border in an 'impressive Hispano-Suiza coach, all chrome and luxurious'. The French guards passed them through to the Spaniards, who welcomed them to the music of the 'Internationale'.

It took Sid Quinn some time too to persuade the Communist Party to send him to Spain, but he was on his way by 26 November 1936: 'They let me go in the end – I'm a stubborn bugger.' On the way he met George Nathan. 'You'll hear a lot about him, of course. He really stood out. He was a real army officer. I think he'd been processed by King Street, but I'm not sure. Although he was travelling on his own we were sure he was going the same way as us. He was a strange man. He'd been a guards officer and was supposed to have had a dubious career in Ireland, but I don't know anything about that.

'I was processed in Paris by some kind of Frenchified chap who was awkward, but the poor bastard was assassinated two days later by the French fascists.' From then on his journey to Spain was similar to that of Maurice Levine, except for an uncomfortable time on the border. 'There was some kind of hold-up at the frontier. We'd all had a huge nosh-up with lots of wine and we found we had to stay on the coach for fourteen hours – we were in *agony* . . .'

The early arrivals continued, usually without trouble. George Aitken 'just got straight through, I'd no trouble at all'. With the tightening up of restrictions following the non-intervention policy, the border was then officially closed and the only routes remaining were those over the mountains.

Mountaineering had not featured largely in the education of the working-class men who went to Spain, and certainly climbing mountains by night is an experience they have never forgotten.

Fred Copeman had decided to go to Spain because 'anyway it would make my girl proud of me and I'd intended to go. So I went along to King Street and they said you're just in time, we've 450 comrades leaving in the morning. I said all right, so here I am – now what happens? They told me all about the weekend ticket and the big café in Paris and from there we went down to the Pyrenees.

'God, when we arrived at the Pyrenees . . . I'd never climbed before in my bloody life. Every mountain you climbed there was another bugger . . . You wondered when the hell you were going to get there.'

Joe Norman went to Paris on his weekend ticket 'with just the clothes I stood up in. I wore an old pair of flannels, a khaki shirt, a button-top sweater and plimsolls. We got to Paris and floated around for days from one hiding place to another as the French had orders to put us in gaol if they found us. Eventually we struggled down to the Pyrenees. Our guides came for us on a bitterly cold night. We evaded the police and climbed in dead silence and in total darkness for eight hours. I've never been so glad to see anything as the sun coming over the brow of the mountain.'

Joe Norman was lucky in that he was allowed to climb in his plimsolls. The others had to exchange whatever footwear they had, however good, for rope-soled espadrilles as these were very quiet and left no footprints. But sizes were random and some men walked out of theirs and finally arrived barefoot, while others struggled on, squeezed into shoes that were far too small.

By the time Charles Morgan set off in 1937 with his party, 'Victoria Station was thick like flies with special agents and detective men looking for people like us. You could tell which they were by their huge feet.

'We were a nondescript crowd. Hardly any of us had any decent clobber as we'd mostly been unemployed. We were told not to say where we were going or what we were doing, but it was all a bit daft. If anyone said are you going to Spain and we'd said yes we'd have been arrested. It wasn't illegal, though, to go to Paris, but we hardly looked right. In those days if you were out of work then you'd no proper suit. Your jacket was one material and your trousers another and you were a bit gaunt. It looked pretty incongruous to be bloody going to Paris.

'I mean *Paris*, of all places . . . it meant oo-la-la and raised eyebrows if you said Paris in those days.' His batch missed their English food – 'They were a bit surprised to get a French breakfast, you know, dainty little rolls and croissants and things' – but one comrade did manage to lose his virginity in a French brothel – 'though that's another and a long story'. Charles also had a fracas with a French taxi-driver who thought he was going to fight for Franco. After hauling him out of his cab, the Frenchman discovered his mistake, asked 'a thousand pardons, why they always do it in thousands I can't think', and delivered him to the Place de Combat free. Perhaps typically of Charles, while at this time everyone else was clambering over the rocks and mountain paths, he swept in by road. 'They just kind of let us through.'

Bill Feeley struggled over the mountains and found it 'a

33

terrific ordeal. I hope I never find myself doing anything like it again.

'We'd been divided into groups. Some went to Carcasonne and some to Lisieux as we knew we might get into trouble with the police. I nearly didn't get as far as the border. A few of us got off at the wrong station and had real problems with no languages at all. Finally we got a lift on a Chevrolet pick-up and we all crammed on somehow with one chap astride the bonnet. We were all waving and cheering, it was like a circus. It were more fun than a picnic . . . We got together again to cross the border and some lads were missing. One had disappeared in Paris.'

It was a rugged route. Sometimes the men had to carry their weaker companions.

But perhaps the prize for sheer effort should go to Bob Doyle. He had tried to volunteer from Ireland but was told he was too young. 'I wasn't satisfied. I decided that if they wouldn't let me go to Spain officially, then I'd go under my own steam. In 1936 I got to London and found a job in Lyons Corner House in Piccadilly – like Ho Chi Minh. I was beating a trail he was to follow later.

'I earned some money and that took me to Jersey where I picked potatoes, and when I thought I'd got enough cash together to get to Spain I found a boat going to Marseilles and took that. I then waited around in Marseilles to find a boat going to Spain I could stow away on, but it took some time. I ended up begging food off ships and sitting all day over a coffee or a shandy in a waterfront café. I slept out under railway wagons at night. I spoke no French at all – it was real hoboing.

'Anyway, finally a ship arrived going to Spain and I stowed away in the anchor room. I was found four hours out from Marseilles. I was taken to the officer who told me that Britain had a non-intervention policy towards Spain and that as soon as the ship reached Valencia I would be arrested. I spent the trip talking to the crew and trying to win their support. When we got to Valencia, as the ship was tying up, I jumped off and ran up the quay, but, of course, I was caught by the police. They handed me over to the British Consul, and I told him I was on my way to join the International Brigade and would he let me go.

'He said there was no such thing. This was at the beginning of 1937. He said what English there were in Spain were hiding around "like rats". He said I would have to work my passage back to Britain and then I'd be arrested. He then let me go for a few hours. So I went off and found a ship where a Spanish lad had jumped ship and they signed me on as a member of the crew. I made several trips after that, in the ship, alternately to Franco and Republican Spain. So far as I can remember we delivered steel sheets to both and brought fruit and wine out. I went to Cádiz and other ports in Franco Spain, and there was always a German presence about. There were two battleships in Cádiz when I was there once, taking out German wounded. Local people didn't like the Germans. They'd come into shops and cafés and take what they wanted and throw people out.

'Anyway, the first time I got leave I went to King Street and told them that if they didn't get me into Spain to fight I'd jump ship anyhow at Alicante.

'They said no, leave properly. As I could speak Spanish by this time I was asked to help by taking a party of volunteers over with me. So I did the Paris trip with the others on weekend tickets, but I had a passport and a seaman's discharge book so I could go anywhere.

'The sixteen members of my party got a bit hectic. They drank a lot and sang revolutionary songs and so on and I told them to shut up. They didn't listen so I ended up by isolating myself from them. When we got to Dunkirk the CID were waiting and took them all on one side. When I got off the boat they asked me where I was going, and I said Paris, but they couldn't do much as I had all the proper documents. They said was I sure I wasn't going east, to Spain, and I said of course not. So I went to Paris and was just able to catch a train, but before I did I had to go and give some kind of explanation as to what had happened to the other sixteen people. Later on, every single one turned up in Spain –

they'd all got back by devious routes.

'Finally I got down to Carcasonne in the Pyrenees. Our party was led by a trapper and we had to dodge the fascist patrols a lot by this time. They were being helped by right-wing French sympathizers and it was all very difficult. They did all they could to prevent us getting over the border, but we finally made it and our first Spanish meal was bread and hot coffee in the trapper's hut."

6   Early Days

The first major confrontation of the war took place in the battles in and around Madrid. They began in the summer of 1936 with a series of Nationalist attacks on the capital which were intended to finish the Republic quickly. In practice it did not work out like that. From the battles on the outskirts of the city itself, such as that of University City, to those in the small towns around the capital, it was a muddled and protracted business. Neither side was either well organized or prepared, and there was still considerable in-fighting going on within the ranks of both. Small groups from each side fought each other, often without contact or liaison or any coherent strategy, and there was a good deal of free-lance activity. The Nationalist general Mola coined a phrase which was to come down the years. When asked which of his four columns would take Madrid, he answered, 'The Fifth Column – of secret Nationalist supporters within the city.' He was wrong. A few of our volunteers saw the ear-liest fighting around the capital and a handful fought in the early battles in the townships nearby, such as Lopera and Las Rozas. 'Here,' says Robert Colodny in *The Struggle for Madrid*, 'were created the myths which plague the historian.'

*

Almost all the volunteers to Spain spent their early days at Albacete, half-way between Madrid and Valencia, where they had what training was available. In the early days it was practically non-existent, but this did improve in time.

There was no XVth Brigade or British Battalion when the first volunteers reached Albacete – that was to come later. The earliest arrivals of all, including the poet John Cornford, had already fought in the battles around Madrid, including that of University City. The fight for Madrid dragged on through the autumn until mid-November.

The next main offensive took place at the very end of the year in the villages around Boadilla and Lopera and in the north-west at Las Rozas. In another attempt to take Madrid, Franco's forces began trying to cut off the Republicans in the Guadarramas and to surround Madrid from the north. One of the main objectives was to cut the Madrid–Corunna road.

By just before Christmas 1936 there were about 150 Britons in Spain, and these became the No. 1 Company under the command of George Nathan. They fought as part of the Marseillaise Battalion of the XIVth Brigade. The commander of the Marseillaise was Major Gaston Delasalle. He was later to be described as 'a coward, a fool and a rigid disciplinarian', and he was also alleged to have been a fascist spy.

The campaign which began on Christmas Eve was designed to provide a diversion to Franco's attack on Madrid by trying to take the village of Lopera, held by the Nationalist forces. Major Delasalle directed operations from safety in the rear and it all became total confusion. He gave repeated orders to attack to the British company, who again and again found themselves walking into a wall of fire. Delasalle provided no support. Casualties were very high and would have been even worse without the efforts made by Nathan, who finally ordered his men to retreat from what had become known as the 'English Crest'.

The experiences of those who arrived first are significant because they were to form part of a pattern which was to be repeated throughout the war: that of the untrained, ill-prepared volunteer being flung into battle at the deep end and of the British being used again and again as the shock troops for an assault. As we will see, they were affected in

38

different ways.

Training had been almost non-existent for the men who went into action at Lopera. When Walter Greenhalgh arrived at Albacete he received none at all. 'We just didn't have any. As soon as we arrived we were told we were going to the front but we'd no idea where. I was detailed off with somebody else to go and pick up some uniforms. We collected a truck which was loaded with clothing, all sorts just thrown together.

'These ranged from ski suits to ex-Spanish, French or Belgian army clothing. There was no order, just a great pile of clothing, so all the lads had to gather round and sort themselves out something that would fit.' Walter had been hanging on to his most precious possession – a blue serge suit – 'but it had to go so I made a present of it to a Spaniard I'd become friendly with and he was highly delighted in spite of the fact that it was all covered with mud, but we didn't actually see any weapons at all until we got to the front near Lopera. We went down by train to a railhead just outside Lopera at Andujar and were sent to a sort of garage place where there were boxes of weapons.

'They were real ancient ones. What I got was an old German gun dated 1878. It was a single-loader. There was a great big pile of cartridges on the floor, not in clips, just in a big heap. What you did was to just pick out handfuls and see if they would fit the breach. You put them in one at a time to see if they'd fit. They were all different kinds – some rimless, some rimmed. I'm sure the gun I had would never have fired anyway.

'This must have been the day before Christmas Eve. We marched out of the town that night with our very odd assortment of weapons, and that night we slept in some orange groves near by. The weather made it hard. During the day it was really hot like an English summer, but during the night it was very, very cold and froze.

'Then I started talking to an elderly Irishman and he had a sort of automatic similar to a Lewis or Sten gun with a magazine which was a quadrant and the bullets were pushed against a large W-spring. I told him that in my army territorial training I had actually fired a Lewis gun, and he said, "Good, you can come with me and be my No. 2." No. 2 is the one who loads the new magazines as No. 1 fires them off.

'So I slung around my neck about ten of these magazines, horrible heavy things they were too, and the next morning we got into trucks and moved off towards Lopera. We got machine-gunned on the way by an aircraft and had our first casualty, a man named Cohen. He fell on top of me. We arrived somewhere along the road in the later afternoon and we were told to jump out and run through this olive grove. We came to the edge of the grove and facing us was a big hill. They told us the fascists were on top of the hill and we had to go and knock them off.

'So, yelling like a load of dervishes we dashed up this hill. They just sat up there and waited and fired their machine guns at us. Every now and then Paddy lies down and fires the gun three or four times, then it would jam and I'd take the thing apart and sort it out and then he'd fire another three or four rounds. It was all very slow.

'But we did finally reach the top without too many casualties and actually chased the fascists away. George Nathan encouraged us throughout. He was such a character with his high boots and he'd brought his officer's uniform with him and he'd a tiny moustache, all neatly curled, and his swagger cane, and he stood there so calmly saying, "All right, lads, away you go." Come to think of it, it was really stupid picture-book stuff. That night, not long after we took the top, it grew dark, and while we were resting George Brown's brother, Mick, who had come out with me came over and said, "This isn't war, it's bloody massacre ... I've had enough," and I never saw him again. He went back to England.

'That was where we lost Ralph Fox. He went off to reconnoitre something and never came back. We never did know what really happened to him. That was where John Cornford was killed too.'

There are many myths about the death of Cornford. But

only Greenhalgh claims to have actually seen what happened.

'I was with John when he was killed. That was the next morning. We were told to advance under cover of darkness before dawn, to within sight of the village of Lopera. We did this. We went down from our high hill, across a valley and up over another hill, and we could see down in the next valley the village of Lopera. We were to wait there until the artillery started firing and then we were to go forward, shouting and running like mad like the night before.

'We were all lying in a long straight line on the brow of the hill and there were three of those veterans who had fought in Madrid. John Cornford was one, Jock Cunningham another, and I can't remember the third. But John had a bandage round his head – he looked like Lord Byron.

'The bandage was very white and he wouldn't wear a hat, and he's up there and I'm on the other side as I was also acting as Nathan's runner. We were waiting for this artillery barrage to open up and nothing happened, everything was quiet, and we could see the fascists coming out of the village, taking their machine-guns along both sides of us, and we are still waiting and still nothing happens. We wait and wait and finally John Cornford climbs up to the brow of the hill to look over and the early sun just catches his white bandage and that was it. He got one straight through the head. That one shot was the beginning of the machine-guns to open on either side of us.

'Nothing happened from our side at all, and there we were about half a mile in front of our own lines with machine-guns on either side of us. Then the artillery opened up, and either ours were firing short or they were firing accurately, but anyway, between us and safety was a huge field which was being blown to pieces.

'We were called back and on the way my Irish friend was very seriously wounded and I managed to get back with him, but it was all total confusion. We had to retreat and the fascists advanced and we even lost that bit of hill we'd taken the night before.'

41

Again, several of our men, as we will see, saw something of the last days of a man whose true motivation remains a mystery.

'That was the incident after which the commander, Delasalle, was said to be a fascist spy.

'Was he? I don't know. I talked to several people that time and one of those I attached myself to was a Dutchman called Piet Jansen. He was a sea captain and a great linguist. He spoke Russian and Chinese and most European languages. He and I were sharing a hole in the ground. He was away all one day, and when he came back he said he was doing some interpreting and that there was a trial and that the commanding officer was being charged with treason.

'He'd been seen going over to the fascist lines and he'd been seen coming back from the fascist village while we were all being shelled. This trial went on for two days, and then Piet came back and said, "He's dead. He was found guilty and one comrade just went up behind him and shot him through the head." ' (His guard at the time was Maurice Levine, whose account comes later.)

'From Lopera we went to Las Rozas, north-west of Madrid. We went straight into action again, but this was a different kind of thing. The Lopera thing was just a skirmish between two small groups, but in Las Rozas we were part of a huge battle which was going on. It was on the second day of it that I got wounded. I got a bullet right through my neck. I think somewhere you might find my name on a roll of honour because for a long time I was considered dead.

'I managed to drag myself off the field. They put a bandage round me and said, "Make your way to the road." I'd been able to walk at first, but then I collapsed on the way. I was picked up by an ambulance driver who took me to Dr Tudor Hart's hospital in Madrid. He said he'd seen me lying on the road and picked me up. He spoke bad Spanish and turned out to be English, and he said I was the first Englishman he'd picked up. All the rest were French or German. That's the last thing I remember of Las Rozas. Apparently they took me away and operated on me, and the next thing I remember was waking up in a hospital bed in a hotel which had been turned into a hospital.'

Sid Quinn arrived at the fort of Figueras first on his arrival in Spain. 'All those Brigaders who were there at the same time will remember what it was like – the excrement lying dotted all over the place. There were thousands of men using it and no proper lavs and it stunk to high heaven. We had our first Spanish meal there, beans in oil with no meat. Then we got to Albacete which had been a base built for 400 cavalry men and 4,000 men were using it. That was absolute chaos too until some Germans arrived and cleaned it up.' His viewpoint differs as he had been a regular soldier and had preconceived ideas.

'We went from there to Madrigueras where we had a bit of basic training, mainly things like forming threes and so on, a continental thing. They tried to knock you into shape in a few days. There were about forty or fifty in my batch including Maurice Levine. We were all pretty raw.

'It was totally different from being a regular soldier. We'd no proper uniforms or anything. We went into action with what gear we had on, as we were, although you could be shot on sight without a uniform. I remember Ralph Fox looked very dashing. He was our commissar. He wore a black beret, black leather coat and a large revolver – very dashing. Then there was young John Cornford, a real romantic type, six foot tall, twenty years of age, and he looked like a bloody Greek god. He'd been at the siege of University City with Jock Cunningham.

'On our way to the front at Lopera I saw the first casualty of the war. He was called Cohen. We were strafed by a plane and a bullet tore a hole in him the size of a football.

'We stopped at a grain warehouse full of sacks of beans. It was bitterly cold that night. We got some ammunition up and I was told, as I'd been a regular soldier, to carry some, and got myself lumbered with carrying 600 rounds. I wore it slung round my neck. I was also carrying my rifle, and as I'd no sleep the night before I felt pretty shattered. Then we came under attacking fire. Ralph Fox came running back to where I was struggling with the ammunition saying, "Come on, get moving." I was like a camel moving up. We got closer and closer until we were under small-arms fire.

'When I turned round Ralph Fox had disappeared, I just saw his toes sticking up. The rule of war is don't go back and help a comrade – you must go forward and leave the stretcher bearers to pick up the wounded. Kit Conroy in his IRA leggings was dashing about telling us to stay here, go there. He was just like the rest of us – he knew nothing about it, but his heart was good through and through, and his courage. Jock Cunningham, like myself, had no uniform, and there he was saying, "Just keep yer heads down, the now . . ." One or two fellows who had been in the First War were taken with violent trembling because they knew what we were in for, they'd been through it. It's always bad before it happens, whether it's the first time or the fifty-first . . . once you get in it's okay.

'The first was really terrific, blasting past your head. But we couldn't just stick it out in a hole, we'd come to fight. So Nathan stood up and said, "Spread out thinly and take a position on the crest of that hill." He'd that famous stick out – it's etched on my mind – pointing it directly here and there saying, "There, go there," and then the position completely changed. We took some ground and held it. We came to a village that had been held by Moors and Italians, and there were hundreds of bodies lying in the street.

'Later we were smoked out and had to take another position. We found the Franco-Belge had broken on the left. We held on for some time and then Maurice and I left to go on a special mission. We were told later that we'd held an advance down into southern Spain, otherwise they'd have smashed their way down to Córdoba.

'Early in the dawn Nathan had come and said to Maurice and me, "There's a lot of our boys down behind the lines. Don't threaten them, just get them to come back. It's understandable." They'd run face to face into a wall of fire, untrained and unseasoned, right into the full attack of the Moors. I talked most of them into coming back. It was during this action that John Cornford was killed, a tragic loss. Him and Fox, too. As well as Fox and Cornford, a lot of men lost their lives there. It was a damned disgrace that they did. After the fight for Lopera we were told to pack up and move to Las Rozas as there had been a fascist break-through.

'That was where I first saw women in action. The Spanish women went out with their men in defence of the line. You remember such odd things. In the heat of the battle at Lopera when we were getting shot at from arsehole to breakfast time, the bloke next to me turned round and said, "What do you think of Arsenal's chances on Saturday?" I said, "Chelsea will bloody murder them." '

Maurice Levine also went into action first on that fated Christmas Eve. 'For this action we were equipped, by the way, with rifles which bore the date 1888 which we'd unpacked out of dirty, greasy rags from old packing cases. They'd probably been bought off gun-runners or something like that. We never had proper clips. We could only fire one round at a time. They were really antique, they were. We had no anti-aircraft guns, no artillery. We just went along there with a few heavy machine-guns and rifles to help stem the advance. We'd had a small amount of rudimentary training, route marches and so on, but ammunition was very scarce and couldn't be spared for practice. I do believe there was one practice of five rounds per man, but I didn't have the pleasure of practising as I happened to spend a short time in prison having been disciplined by Delasalle, and during that period they had the practice. So I personally fired my first shot of any kind at Lopera.'

(Maurice had been detailed off to guard the cookhouse of the French commander and seeing the quality of the food had persuaded the cooks to give him some. Delasalle found out and sent him to prison for a week.)

'I was with a French machine-gun team, as a rifleman and carrier of ammunition. But after a day all the British were taken away as we had language difficulties and we became No. 1 Company, on our own. I fought throughout Lopera, and was then sent to Las Rozas to hold up the advance of the fascist forces. We passed through Madrid and Nathan told us that we had two hours off to look at Madrid, and then we moved to Las Rozas to hold up the fascists.

'Although we didn't know it at the time, this was to be the famous battle of the Corunna road. It was very arduous fighting in the foothills of the mountains at 2,000 and 3,000 feet. We stayed there until the end of January, and then the remnant of the British left from the Lopera and Las Rozas actions joined up with the new British Battalion which was being formed at Madrigueras. By this time hundreds had followed us to Spain. When we joined the battalion with Nathan there were only 45 of us left of the 150 that went to Lopera, the rest were dead, wounded or sick. We were the veterans and we went off then to the Jarama front where we were dug in from the middle of February until mid-June.

'Was I frightened of going into action? I wasn't too frightened at first because it was night-time the first time and I couldn't see anything. Just flashes of fire a little distance away. I wasn't afraid then, but the next morning, when we moved to a new position on the hill, I saw dead lying round and I did get a shock, seeing those dead people. I'd never seen a dead person before. You could see where the bullets had entered through their chest or somewhere and then blown its way out.

'The time I was most frightened came a day or so later. That evening, just as we had used our helmets to dig a few inches of hole in the ground to give some cover against fire, Peter Kerrigan and General Walter arrived and asked me and my companion, who was Sid Quinn, to do a job for him. He wanted us to escort and guard the commander of the Franco-Belge back to the rear and stay the night at a certain farmhouse. "Don't sleep, and watch your prisoner," he said. "In the morning you will deliver Colonel Delasalle to Divisional Headquarters." We did, and we understand he was court-martialled next day and shot. We were told he was shot through the head as he left the room. We asked George Nathan, who was there, why had the commander been executed, and he said he'd been found guilty of incompetence, cowardice and being a spy. It was later said that Delasalle had admitted to being a regular officer in the French army and had worked as a spy against the Soviet Union during his time as a military attaché in Bucharest.

'Anyway, we returned to the olive grove and slept heavily as we'd missed the previous night's sleep. The next morning we woke about six and it was very, very quiet. During the night the whole front had changed and the French and British had moved to a new front.

'I walked over to the next olive tree which had been Nathan's HQ and got an awful shock. It had been abandoned. Near to it was a little bivouac which contained two corpses of men who looked as if they'd been dead a couple of days.

'I realized everyone had left, and that was when I got really frightened. I couldn't walk – my legs just wouldn't move. I crawled back to Sid who'd been a regular soldier and said, "They've gone, I think they've advanced." He knew more about it than me, having recently been thrown out of the army for being a communist. "Don't be bloody silly," he said. "Advance? – the buggers have retreated!" He said if there'd been an advance there would have been supplies and troops moving up. "There's been a sodding retreat. Come on, let's get out of it," he said.

'All we knew was that the sun set behind the fascist lines so we walked away from the sun all day. We'd had nothing to eat the previous day and all we could find was oranges, which we ate, peel and all. Strangely enough we were walking the right way.

'At dusk we saw a patrol on the road and didn't know if they were Spaniards or Moors as they were very dark-skinned. We were hiding in the plantations on the side of the road because we didn't know where we were or whether they were the enemy or Republicans. We decided to wait until dark and hang on until we could hear people's voices and what language they were speaking.

'Actually they were speaking Spanish, which didn't help

much, and Sid said, "Come on, let's get it over with." I didn't much fancy getting shot there and then. If you were taken prisoner it was odds on what happened. Some were all right, others were shot out of hand as an example. Anyway, they were in fact Republicans, and we'd walked to the exact village which the British No. 1 Company had retired to.

'It was all just by chance. We met Nathan as soon as we got there and he said he'd given us up for dead.'

7 The Support Services

The battles around the city of Madrid itself had come to an end by mid-autumn. Christmas and the New Year saw the battles in the nearby townships and on the Corunna road, which were to be followed by savage fighting on the Jarama river in the early spring of 1937. During this period two other volunteers arrived who were to be involved in a different way. Albert Cole fought with the Spanish navy and Will Paynter came out to take over as political commissar. Walter Greenhalgh, partially recovered from the wound he received at Lopera, became a courier. The work of these three men was to continue against the bigger canvas of the war in general and concurrently with those taking part in the battles which were to follow.

Albert Cole was one of the handful of volunteers who went into the Spanish Republican navy. He was approached about going to Spain because of his work in the National Unemployed Workers' Movement and he said, 'I'd love to but I'd be no use, I've never been in the army only in the navy. They said it would be good for morale if I joined the navy there.

'A week later myself, Jack Coward and four other Liverpudlians were told we could go. We'd all been in the navy and we did the usual trip to Paris, the weekend tickets and so on, and then got down to the border and climbed the Pyrenees and I hope I never have such an experience again.

'When we reached the headquarters at Albacete they were sending everyone to the front in batches. We were the last British left and I remember although we were tired out Jack

49

Coward got us to do physical exercises in the bull ring.

'We were sent down to Cartagena, the naval base, the Republican navy headquarters. I was put in charge of a torpedo boat. They had one cruiser, the *Libertad*, and two or three destroyers. Our job then – it was the middle of December 1936 – was to make sure the transporter ship delivered its goods and that no submarines got into the harbour. Because of the non-intervention policy we could do very little. Otherwise we would have gone as far as North Africa and refuelled in Gib., but we couldn't take on enough fuel to do the journey there and back.

'It was all designed to keep morale going more than anything else. The Spanish crew weren't like British sailors. It was all, "*Mañana, mañana*" – tomorrow, tomorrow – and I'd shout and say, "Not *tomorrow*, NOW," and try and make them do it my way. They were very easy-going like that, even the officers.

'We never even saw any subs. We'd patrol across from cape to cape for twenty-four hours and then be relieved for twenty-four. It never stopped. We were bombed a few times, and so was the transporter, but not often.

'I remember us taking a ship full of refugees and shells up north. They painted a big Union Jack on the side to fool the fascists and I realized it was upside down. I knew it would be a dead giveaway. So I made them do it again.

'I then stood on the bridge, smoking a pipe and looking like a British captain. When we were stopped by fascist gunboats and asked why we were around, I managed to keep going on a string of plausible tales. When asked about cargo I said we were in ballast, but once said the wrong word which meant explosives instead – which was right – but they just thought I was an idiot and didn't take me up on it.

'When we got nearer France we hung over the side and painted out the Union Jack and painted on a French flag in case we ran into British gunboats and they got too nosy. We delivered 2,000 refugees to Bordeaux and left the ship there, after which I got two months' leave back in Britain.

'I got papers, saying I was a commercial traveller, from

the Spanish Consul. I had a Spanish passport as well as a British one as all those who fought in Spain for the Republic were given Spanish citizenship and were told Spain was their homeland too.

'I felt disappointed as I'd seen virtually no action at sea. We were once sent off to help clear a road to a village which had been bombed, and the fascist planes came along and fired on all the helpless refugees on the roadside, even the little children and babies. That was the worst thing I saw myself.

'After I got back to Spain from leave, the country had been cut in two and there was nothing for us to do in the navy so I asked to be redrafted and I ended up in the Abraham Lincoln Battalion of the XVth Brigade – the Americans.

'Food wasn't too good there. You'd rub a bit of onion on some bread and eat that. We smoked poppy leaves and dried lettuces – lettuce was best – but we fought very hard. We were lucky, I think, not to get too much political chat in the Abe Lincoln. By the time you'd fought all day, then taken your gun to pieces and cleaned it and put it together again, there wasn't much time for political discussions. You were glad just to sleep. I remember going to one big meeting, though, when La Pasionaria said it was better to die on your feet than live on your knees.

'Then I got wounded. Those same transporters I'd worked to protect used to bring in nice little anti-tank guns for a three-man crew. We were using one near an ammunition dump when a shell hit the dump and blew us all up. The Americans were blown to pieces. I was in hospital for over a month. While we were there local people were so desperate they'd eat what we'd left even if it had been chewed. We did have some Red Cross parcels, though, and had about 350 pesetas a month pay, but I gave mine away. You couldn't buy anything with it and it wasn't worth carrying around.

'I suppose I was there most of the war, December 1936 until I was sent to hospital on 14 October 1938. I was in hospital until 16 November. Just after I came out I was sent north to be repatriated, and there I finally met Sam Wild who was commander of the British Battalion by that time. I always remember it. He'd caught a chap red-handed pilfering and he got him out in front of everyone, ripped off his IB badge, took away any other signs he'd been in the IB, and then handed him over to an IB escort to be taken away. He was quite right.

'Sam liked discipline. I remember, too, a Yank going through and banging a door where Sam was and Sam shouted for him to come back. He wouldn't so Sam went and yanked him back and made him shut the door properly.

'During those times at sea, though, I thought a lot about why I was there as we went back and forth, back and forth. I was about 100 per cent Tory when I was young and I went into the navy as a very young lad. Then on one trip we went to Vladivostock, and got frozen up in the ice for three months. While I was there I went to some lectures and they really got hold of me. I remember one girl lecturer talking about India and I said, "Why should we have to give India up when it makes us so much money?" and she said, "Why, how much money do you have sunk in India?" It made me think that the only thing I'd ever give to India was my blood if I got sent there to get killed defending it. Another chap asked her if she believed everyone was equal and would she go out with a Chinaman or sleep with one – he were a cheeky bugger, really – and she said, "Actually I'm married to one." There was a lot about the political system in Russia I didn't like, but I ended up a founder member of the CP in Liverpool.

'But after Spain I never got active in the party again.'

Will Paynter, as we have seen, was already a leading figure in the NUM. In March 1937, following the heavy fighting around Madrid and the protracted campaign on the Jarama, it was decided to send him out to Spain to look after the interests of the British Battalion at the headquarters of the International Brigade and to deal with problems which might arise.

He did not go, he admits, with very great enthusiasm as he had not long been married and was concerned about his young wife – a concern which was to be justified when she died in childbed giving birth to twins.

However, he followed the usual route to Spain, the week-end ticket to Paris – although he was closely questioned on the boat by plain-clothes policemen – and the train to the Pyrenees. He, too, climbed the mountains overnight in the rope-soled shoes.

'Although I was going out as a political commissar I had a week's basic training at Figueras in an old fort. This mostly consisted of teaching us how to run under fire, marching – which was supposed to develop our physical fitness – and that was about it. There was no arms training as there were no rifles.

'From there I went down to Albacete where I relieved Wally Tapsell who'd been political commissar before me. Wally, who'd been circulation manager of the *Daily Worker*, then went up to Catalonia where the Nationalists staged a *putsch* which was quickly defeated by the Republican forces.

'In spite of my title as political commissar I ended up seeing a lot of the action. It turned out to be a job where I was not just stuck at Albacete, I had to get out and deal with all sorts of problems. These included differences within the leadership and the problems arising from the situation of the lads who volunteered. You see, they weren't getting paid so there was no money coming back to the families. They were receiving pathetic letters from home about difficulties and straitened circumstances and when were they coming home?

'Part of my job was to deal with that. I had to emphasize the politics of the struggle which was taking place. The other thing was that the fascists were so much better equipped to wage war – their standard of technology, the sheer number of arms and the kind of arms they had and their aircraft – and efforts had to be made to get what we could. We got a

53

certain number of arms from Russia and some on the black market – there's always a black market on that kind of thing – but the non-intervention policy meant there was always a shortage and that didn't help morale.

'Then there were the problems of the lads who'd been in the trenches in the Jarama for week after week and month after month, and really the situation on that front was stalemate. Well, they ended up spending weeks of time with no activity but the occasional spurt of rifle fire, and I had to keep going up there to try and get them withdrawn for some rest. I tried to get them out if only for a day or two to a village where they could get a drink and a few hours of a different kind of life.

'But of course you couldn't withdraw men unless there were replacements and that was the difficulty. It was bad on morale.

'Then in the July came the Brunete offensive aimed at taking the pressure off Madrid. It was very costly as far as human life was concerned – in the British Battalion particularly. Some very good lads were killed in that. The battles were ferocious, there was no effective support after the first attack and there was tremendous disorganization which obviously led to a lowering of morale and some lads just walked away altogether.

'It was all right at the beginning of the battle when they did have some support from artillery and aircraft, but then the fascists attacked on another sector of the front and the British lads found themselves isolated – more or less for target practice. I went up to the front about the sixth day and the whole thing was a hell of a mess.

'There'd been some desertions – lads had desperately tried to get home. Some managed it, they got away on an onion boat or something, but others were arrested and brought back to prison in Albacete. I'm not saying there were a lot of people who deserted, but there were some and I had to intercede on their behalf. The penalty for desertion in any army is harsh, but together with Americans from the Abraham Lincoln Battalion who were having similar problems I pressed the brigade to set up a centre where those who had weakened could be rehabilitated.

'The camp was set up, but at first the lads wouldn't listen to me or anybody else. I went there with Arthur Horner and I'll never forget the experience. We had a meeting, but the lads showed no interest at all until Arthur started to describe the Tommy Farr–Joe Louis fight . . . I had to talk my way out of a really difficult position and explain the problems of repatriation, the reasons for the camp and the alternatives they would have had to face had I not pressed for it. It was a while before their anger and bitterness subsided, but eventually, after some weeks there, most of the men went back to the battalion refreshed and in good spirits.

'Then, too, I had to see the wounded in hospital and see what could be done to make their lot easier. There were some terrible cases. I remember Jack Brent who was in continuous pain, in agony, a bullet had caught him on the base of the spine – he's dead now. Then there was another fellow, the son of a professor or something, he'd been running and ducking and a bullet had sliced off the top of his head, there was an enormous hole, and he was so anxious to do another job as he could speak Spanish and French. Yet there he was with this terrible wound which they didn't have the facilities to deal with or even to cover it properly.'

A number of British volunteers were down on the Córdoba front, and the British had been pressing for them to be returned to the battalion. Will was given the task of taking down some Italian volunteers and bringing the British lads back.

'We travelled down through Spain in a big truck, sleeping and waking, breathing in the clouds of dust from the road, eating and drinking sparsely depending on what we'd managed to bring with us from base. I don't remember all the details, but I do remember the magnificent country around Ciudad Real. The round trip took five long, tiring days and at the end of it I was so tired that when I got to the hotel in Madrid – which only had a room because it was within shelling range of the fascist lines – I slept through everything, including a bombardment during which the hotel porch was blown off by a shell. I never heard a thing.

'In September the battalion was moved to Belchite where a new attack was developed, and again they were in the thick of the fighting. The new battalion commander, Peter Daly, was killed there. He was one of the men I had brought back from Córdoba, and I had some responsibility too for his being made commander. He was typical of the men who were the backbone of the battalion.

'I was constantly moving between the base and the front line, dealing with the massive problems following so many casualties. I was travelling once with a number of men who were returning to the battalion, including Malcolm Dunbar, a fine man and soldier, who had just recovered from a wound in the neck. We were travelling along a straight road in a van when we saw a big lorry approaching which, as it reached us, seemed to swerve. It hit us and we turned over several times before we came to a stop.

'Our driver fell out as it overturned, I went out through the windscreen from the seat beside him, while the men in the back took the full brunt of it. The lorry driver and I escaped except for cuts and bruises, but the men had to be taken to hospital in Benicassim. A heavy vehicle on a straight road with a tired driver was the official explanation for the accident. I passed the spot the next day and the van was useless – it had been stripped clean.

'The Germans were active in Belchite. When we captured their positions we found well-constructed dugouts, some of which contained women's clothing. They had obviously tried to make themselves comfortable, but when I got there it was just an upturned graveyard, with the stench of death from blackened and bloated corpses showing what a bloody battle had been fought.'

Before leaving in the autumn of 1937 – he was recalled by the Communist Party to Britain – he had seen, he says, a vast amount of human suffering. As he wrote in a letter to *Miner's Monthly* in July 1937, the idea of the war, of uniformed soldiers, machine-gun fire and the hum of aeroplanes was only part of the truth. It was a conflict in which masses of men, women and children were forced to take part.

'To see twenty or thirty little children in a small peaceful railway station, fatherless and motherless, awaiting transportation to a centre where they can be cared for, is to get a picture of misery. To see middle-aged and old women with their worldly belongings tied within the four corners of a blanket, seeking refuge from a town or village that has already been bombed, is to get a picture of havoc and desolation. To see long queues of women and children outside the shops patiently waiting for a bit of butter is to get a picture of the privation and suffering entailed.'

Yet, through it all, life went on, 'and it is a common sight to see the peasant farmer working in the olive groves or the ploughed field within the range of rifles or machine-gun fire'.

Will Paynter, because of the job he did in Spain, saw some of the other side, the frightened men who had lost morale, the in-fighting, but he stresses that this was only a small part of the struggle in Spain. 'This was a people's army where self-discipline of a very high order was required, and this, like every human quality, has its moments of weakness as well as its moments of strength. The men had volunteered because they were politically conscious and wanted to help in the fight to defeat fascism. But zeal in support of any cause is a fluctuating condition. It was my job to try and find solutions and remedies for the problems and difficulties which arose.'

But of the incidents he witnessed, one stays in his mind. 'I was returning from the front to a little town called Tortosa. On that summer afternoon as we entered the town we were confronted with the sight of women and children fleeing from it. Out of the air had swept a squadron of fascist planes. Their objective was to bomb a certain railway bridge across the river. The river was dry and we were astounded to see some women with a terrible look of anguish on their faces rushing towards the river bed beneath the course of the planes. There in the dry river bed, playing in the sand, were between twenty and thirty little children. Those children were blown to fragments on that summer afternoon.'

We left Walter Greenhalgh lying in hospital in Madrid, shot through the neck. The wound was effectively to end his career as a fighting soldier, but he managed to find himself a succession of jobs which kept him in Spain for a considerable while longer.

'One day I was visited in hospital by another patient, Tony Larlham, who was a Chelsea artist and a bit of a Bohemian. He'd got it in the leg and couldn't get about much. We became friends and were eventually evacuated to just outside Benicassim. We were the only two Internationals – all the others were Spanish. After a few days, when we could get about, we wandered through the village. It was a kind of seaside place, and Tony actually managed to get *credit* for us in the bars ... He did it on the basis that one day we would get paid for being in the army. I'd never even thought about money until then.

'Then we found out that in the next village were members of the British Battalion with British doctors and wounded, so we transferred. I'll point out that when we did get there, we got a little bit of money and Tony went back to Benicassim and paid our debts.

'The medical unit was run by Dr Sollenberger who I'd known in Manchester when he was working at the Bury Royal Infirmary. It was while we were being looked after in this unit that we heard about the Jarama battle. The British Battalion had been into action and had been very badly decimated. Dr Sollenberger said to us that we could all stay put and read about these things or we could go and see what we could do to help out up there. He said, "I know we're not supposed to, but I know that tonight we can pinch two trucks and we can go." This is what we did – he led us. All of us went and eventually found our way to the Jarama front.

'We ended up at Morata de Tajuña, which was the little

village before the front, and who should be the commander of the base but Piet Jansen, and I was immediately made second-in-command because Piet was working twenty-four hours a day to organize supplies going up to the front. He grabbed me to be his assistant as I wasn't fit to fight – I mean, this was the type of organization it was.

'This may have saved my life. The rest went into an abortive attack and they were nearly all killed. This was the second big battle of the Jarama, the one which settled the front. My comrades were, in fact, nearly all killed that night, including Tony Larlham. They didn't let Dr Sollenberger go to the front, they put him under arrest to prevent him going as doctors were scarcer than soldiers. We tried to explain that there were some who carried guns and some who did not and he was far too valuable. He got killed in the end, though, during the Brunete offensive.

'From then on I had jobs of all kinds to do which never actually took me into the front line. I was Piet's assistant until we moved out of the Jarama and I organized the food going up to the front and made sure that the cookhouse was working and that kind of thing.

'Unfortunately, by the end of the time Piet was going, well, strange. We used to get quite a lot of visitors. We had Hemingway, Harry Pollitt, Professor Haldane. Piet firmly believed that, way out in the wide world, were workers who were working hard for us, even in Germany. He thought that every time a shell was fired at us and didn't explode, that shell must contain a message saying it had been sabotaged by workers in the foreign factories.

'He used to collect these shells and he stored them in the bedroom where we both slept. When Haldane visited us – and Haldane was a mountain of a man – we gave up our beds. I'd been sleeping under the bed and Piet on top of it, but we gave up the arrangement for Haldane. In the middle of the night Haldane loomed in the door and said, "What's that?" So I told him the story of Piet's theory of messages in unexploded shells. "You're mad," he shrieked, "you're all mad ..." We never saw him again. Eventually Piet was taken away and had a complete nervous breakdown. It happened to a few of the people who had got there very early and got no break for a long time. I liked Piet.

'After the Jarama, when there was quite a prolonged rest period, I was taken into the political commissariat with George Aitken and I helped to produce the cyclostyled newspaper called *Our Fight*. I used to take the Spanish newspapers and listen to the radio and pick up bits and pieces. It was all produced in a truck, at night-time, and the first thing we had to do was to get to the front of the truck with towels and drive the clouds of flies out and then drop the canvas down or the flies would have been dropping down over the typewriters all night. Then we'd work all night and take copies of these things up to where the lads were. We managed to get it out every day.

'I ran it myself for a short time, but by then the Americans arrived and they had all the equipment and a team of about fifty to produce their newspaper. When they arrived they looked amazing – they were all got up like First War doughboys.

'Towards the end of that time I was used as a special messenger. Frank Ryan used to send me here and there with parcels. I never knew what it was that was in them. He used to say, "Whatever you do don't let it leave your person." He was a great character was Frank – you know, the kind of gentle Irishman, completely different from the sort of person you'd have thought fought in the early IRA.

'Then we came to the battle of Brunete and so many, many died. George Brown died there – he went straight in and it was his first battle and he was killed on the second or third day. Dr Sollenberger died there too. He was moving up to the front with his truck when it was bombed and he was blown to bits. He'd pioneered surgery at the front. He had this truck with a mobile operating theatre. We were in a truck behind it at the time and we had passed a building which had just been shelled and it fell against the side of our truck. I was standing up pushing the rubble off our truck when the first-aid truck was hit. Then I thought I'd been hit myself as I felt a pain in my hands, but I discovered I'd shoved my hands into a hornets' nest. They came up like footballs.

'After Brunete I left the battalion altogether and worked for a while as a courier going all over the place. Then I became political commissar to a transport unit. One of the jobs I did while I was there was to go into Teruel, immediately after we'd captured it, and pinch all the trucks the fascists had left behind. Unfortunately the cold was so intense they'd all frozen up and we couldn't get them moving.

'I worked with that unit for a while – it was a mixed Italian, Spanish and English unit – right up until the battle of the Ebro. I was on the Ebro until just before it took a turn for the worse, just before the International Brigades were pulled out in the autumn of 1938.'

There were very, very few of his old comrades left. Even after the Jarama 'there weren't many left who came out with me, let alone from those of us who fought at Lopera. Not many came back from our group that went from Manchester. Sam Wild was amazing. He was wounded on the Jarama and went back, at Brunete and went back. He had a charmed life.

'One of the things I've always regretted was that just before the battle of Brunete, George Brown gave me an International Brigades song-book which had all the signatures in of the lads who volunteered from Manchester. He asked me to keep it for safekeeping, and I did for a long time. Then one day there was a Polishwoman and she asked me if she could borrow it for a day to have a look at. I lent it to her and on the same day I was sent off on one of my journeys and I never saw her again. There was every member of the Manchester lot who had fought in Spain up until that time.

'Oddly enough I thought I was not going to get back just once during my time in Spain. I'd gone to Valencia as a courier and was walking down the street when I heard loud Scots voices, you know the way British people talk when they're abroad, and there were these sailors trying to buy playing cards. It turned out they were blockade runners.

'They were intrigued when I went into the shop and tried to help them, because of my odd uniform, and they invited me on to their ship for a meal. Only afterwards have I realized – I was very simple at the time – that they were probably looking for someone to go to bed with. Anyway, they offered me steak and I was only too pleased to go. By the time I finally got away it was midnight and I had to run out of the docks.

'Running along, a couple of men suddenly appeared at the side of me and stuck a gun in my ribs and said, "Come with us." They went on to ask who I was, where had I been, why was I running? It was too dark to see, but they didn't seem to be in uniform. My heart was thumping.

'I didn't know who they were – Republicans, fascists or POUM – there was a lot of trouble with POUM at the time. We went down a dark street and they pushed me into a dark room with one blue light-bulb glowing at the end of it. There was nothing in the room but me and the electric light and them questioning me, and the Spanish was much too difficult for me to follow.

'All the time I had the gun sticking in me and I didn't know who they were. I didn't know whether to take out the pass I carried with me all the time informing everybody that I was a courier. I stuck it out for about three hours and then I got really worried as to what they'd do and showed them my pass. I think they were POUM, I'm not sure. Anyway, they said I could go but by that time I'd missed my transport back to Albacete. Unfortunately, the only thing going my way was a lorry loaded with hides. I hid under them and by the time I arrived back I stank.

8 Jarama

'Death stalked the olive trees
Picking his men
His leaden finger beckoned
Again and again.'
                    — John Lepper, British volunteer

By the spring of 1937, the non-intervention policy pursued by the Western European powers was beginning to bite to the detriment of the Republicans. Three battles were fought during that period: the Nationalists fought over and took Málaga (after which there were the most ferocious and terrible reprisals for Republican sympathizers); there was a second battle around the town of Guadalajara which the Republicans won; and there was the protracted stalemate of Jarama. Jarama presented an almost First World War situation, with both sides, after initial hard fighting, dug into trenches with sporadic activity during which troops were sent over the top. Jarama was yet another attempt by the Nationalists to take Madrid. But while the main Republican effort was centred on fighting them off, the Nationalists continued to be active elsewhere, relentlessly squeezing the Republican enclaves in the north: the Asturias and the Basque country. It was while the stalemate was continuing on the Jarama in April 1937 that the Nationalists bombed Guernica.

*

By the end of December 1936 British volunteers were trickling steadily into Spain, and during January 1937 the British Battalion of the XVth International Brigade came into existence, consisting of approximately 600 men. They were based on Madrigueras. The small remnant of the British No. 1 Company which had fought at Lopera and Las Rozas joined the rest of the battalion there.

The battalion was about to embark on the most protracted campaign of the war, on the Jarama river, to the south-east of Madrid. The object of the Nationalist attack was to capture the Madrid–Valencia road. At the beginning of February 1937 they attacked in the valley of the Jarama with five mobile columns, each with a regiment of Moors, and along with a German Condor Legion armed with new 88-millimetre guns. They drove through all initial opposition and managed to reach the junction of the rivers Jarama and Manzanares, just short of the road junction at Vaciamadrid, which brought the Madrid–Valencia road under their fire.

At dawn on 11 February the Nationalists crossed the Jarama. A group of Moors had worked silently in the dark and crossed to San Martín de la Vega where they knifed the sentries of the French André Marty Battalion (now part of the XIVth Brigade) one by one while they were standing at their posts, thus letting the main body of the force across the river.

The battle proper, which was fierce and bitter, lasted for only four days, and although there was one further attempt by the Nationalists to break through on 27 February, after that initial battle the front was bogged down in a stalemate for months. Both sides were too strong and too well dug in.

The first battle in which the XVth Brigade and the British Battalion fought inflicted massive losses. The XVth Brigade was commanded by Colonel 'Gal' (Janos Galicz, a naturalized Russian who was known for his bad temper), with George Nathan as the British Chief of Staff. The British Battalion was commanded by Tom Winteringham, who had taken over shortly before from Wilfred MacCartney who had been accidentally shot in the leg), and its first political commissar was David Springhall, followed soon by George Aitken.

Again the stories of the volunteers show the lack of preparation for what was to come and the apparent lack of any coherent and overall policy. This is clearly reflected in their own accounts of the lead-up to Jarama and what it was like to take part. Each participant only saw his own part of a confusing and frightening battle, though the individual accounts add up to an overall picture.

The British Battalion bore the brunt of the initial attack. Although the men had not expected to go straight into action, they defended the so-called 'Suicide Hill' for seven hours throughout 12 February, against artillery and machine-gun fire, without maps and with three quarters of the battalion never having held a weapon in their hands before.

The lack of basic training, let alone with weapons, is still a raw subject. 'We were really just left to it at Madrigueras,' said Charles Morgan. 'We had to fend for ourselves. We knew an offensive was coming up but it made no difference. Let's face it, not all the International Brigaders were crusaders – there were unemployed miners from South Wales, men from the Tyneside and the kind of men I've met since who just like a fight and are going to get in one anywhere – you find them all over the world. They've no ties and sometimes they become mercenaries and sometimes idealists, but anyhow they're soldiers born and bred.

'Now what they needed was an explanation of the military and political situation – why they were there. (I knew why I was there, to get the hell out of the dole.) Instead we got lectures, lectures, lectures on Marxism – how many tractors the Soviet Union had produced, how many hectares of wheat were growing in the Ukraine. I rose up in the end and played hell. I screamed – because I do – I said, "We don't want this bloody rubbish. We need training. You want to get us out into the fields and put up sixty- or seventy-pound packs on our back and march us till our balls fall off. We're pleased the Soviet Union is fighting the battle for socialism, but we need to be taught how to fight now, how to take cover, lie doggo, how to march and march until you've reached the point of exhaustion and passed it and you still have to go on. We're not going over the top with a copy of *Das Kapital* in our hands."

'I was told to shut my bleeding gob before someone put a bullet through my head . . . but I was mad. It was all political commissars and no proper officers and chaps'll only obey orders when they have confidence in the bloke that's giving them. Some of those poor bloody lads never even had a chance to fire a shot on the Jarama – they went over the top without training or experience of any kind and were just slaughtered.'

Even later in the campaign training was largely a matter of luck. Garry McCartney, speaking of arriving at the end of the Jarama campaign in June and complaining of his lack of training, was taken up short by another Glaswegian. 'Training, he says. When Garry arrived in June some of our lot who had arrived in April, including me, had been trained, gone to the front, been wounded, sent to hospital, and got back all in those three months.' Scot George Murray said, 'I was told I'd have six weeks' basic training, a concentrated six weeks. I got there one night and was sent off bang on the next, straight up to the front. I'll say it was concentrated all right – concentrated into one day.'

George Aitken, the ex-professional soldier and a participant with some idea of the Republican strategy, gives his account of that first battle. 'We marched into a village near the front, Chinchon, and stayed the night there. Then, during the night or early morning we moved off in lorries to where the attack was going to be launched against the Nationalists on the Jarama. We went straight into action. We spread out across the hills, across the countryside through the olive groves. I think it was getting well into the forenoon before we came in sight of the fascist forces and came under fire. But very soon it became a desperate battle.

'Looking back, I think some of our people were pushed out too far and became isolated, particularly because we were so badly armed. But we managed to hold on during the first day more or less, but then, during the night, Winteringham told me to go and see what was going on at the back and rally up some stragglers and get the food supplies flowing and so on. In the course of that night we got food up to the front – Winteringham says I even brought him his coat.

'On the second morning he asked me to take a group of fifty people away on to the left and try and give the people who were isolated in these forward positions covering fire and draw the fire off them. We were there for some hours, firing on and off, as much as we could, and then we were sent back as the people in front of the main force had been overrun and some taken prisoner.

'We made our way back through the olive groves to this famous sunken road which we were occupying. I remember getting through those olive groves to this day – the fire was tremendous. It was a sheer miracle that I managed to get through. I was running and running and then jumped into the sunken road. When I landed, it was to discover that Winteringham, our commander, was lying there wounded. He'd been shot in the leg so we organized a stretcher party to take him away. This was well on into the second day. The men in front had been overrun, there were virtually no officers left. One man, called Overton, was in the road with the rest of us. He was an ex-guardsman and he told me that as a regular soldier he felt we should retreat as he felt the position was hopeless.

'I refused as our orders from the Brigade were to hold the position until the order was countermanded . . . we had to hold on. He ran up and down the road, still saying we should withdraw. Then about midnight, in the darkness, there was a tremendous explosion. Our ammunition dump had gone up on the part of the road where he was. It is said that he had lobbed a mills bomb in among the ammunition and shouted, "Retire, retire!" and took to his heels followed by a considerable number of men. It was left to me to try and stop the rout.

'I think we managed to prevent the majority from disappearing. By this time we'd lost damn near half the battalion. We'd gone into action over 600 strong and by midnight on the second day we'd lost between 200 and 300 men. Anyway, we finally sent out a patrol, having got some order, to see if there were any signs of the enemy as Overton had been shouting, "The fascists are coming!" It was quite possible, in the darkness of the Spanish night and with the moon shining on the olive groves, to imagine that the trees were men moving. Overton genuinely thought that. Anyway, our patrols couldn't find any.

'Then I sent other patrols out to link up with the main force. Just after dawn Jock Cunningham arrived to take over command. I don't know where he'd been since the night before the battle when we shared a billet. He came from the same part of the country as me, had been a regular soldier in the Argyll and Sutherland Highlanders and had led a mutiny in Jamaica. He was tried, found guilty and sent to the glasshouse where they reckoned they could break anyone, but they didn't break Cunningham. However, by the time he arrived on the scene of the battle his company had been wiped out. He took over and told me to go and round up any stragglers.

'I also tried to get some food up to the front, none had come up. I went behind the lines and found rumours rife that a retreat was taking place. I got a lift down to the base in Morata to find out what the hell was going on, if there was a retreat, but nobody knew anything about it. On my way back to the front I saw a score or more of our people coming down from the front and I told them to get back. I think it was the only time I had my revolver out all the time I was in Spain.

'I said, "There's no retreat, go back, turn round", and they moved off back to the front. By the time I got there and checked with Cunningham he said there'd been some kind of retreat and I told him not so far as I knew. Anyway, our stragglers were marched off by Cunningham back to the front. They spread out over the hills and eventually dug themselves in during the next day or two and established the line. I understand Copeman was busy during the Jarama battle, but I only saw him on the first day.

'After those first three or four days the fascists had shot their bolt. Their losses also were enormous, even though we'd only old rifles. But they didn't pursue their advance once they were stopped. If they had succeeded in cutting the Madrid–Valencia road, it would have been impossible for Madrid to hold out. They didn't succeed then and they never did succeed. There was another attack on the 27th, but by that time the Americans had come up so it wasn't like the first one for us. But they were thrown straight into it, and they had enormous casualties. They tried to force the fascists back across the Jarama river and the attack was a complete failure. For a time there was trouble in the American battalion over it – they felt they'd been thrown into a hopeless fight.'

Fred Copeman's reaction to warfare was far more emotional and subjective. When he arrived on the Jarama to look after a machine-gun unit, 'most of them had been lost, but by the time I arrived we had a dozen Russian Maxims. They're a lovely gun, but you have to know what's what when you use them. They're terrible things to face but beautiful pieces of machinery.

'It was sunrise when we unloaded our gear – clear, clear weather, a lovely day with dogfights in the sky overhead between the Germans and Russians. The Russian planes were like conker boxes, made a hell of a lot of noise but went like hell. It was all rocks where we were until we got down among the olive groves.

'We were in the groves when I heard a little rustle. I'd never heard a gun go off in my life, and there was this little sound, like a leaf dropping from a tree, then two more "leaves", then it got louder and the bloke beside me fell down dead and I thought, God, this is awful, it's bloody awful.

'I got very worried. You know, nuts aren't frightened . . .

your genuine nutter has no fear, battle to him is like a picnic. If you're intelligent you get bloody scared. We got to a slope where there was a sunken road about fifty yards away. Then all hell was let loose and our lads ran down the hill into the valley. There were two little hillocks at the bottom of the valley and I said, "Let's stop here, me old mates." I'd been equipped by my trade union with all the gear, binoculars, compass, Sam Browne belt and what went with it so I was better off than most.

'That rush down the hill ... God, in half an hour 200 of our blokes were dead, you know. That's a hell of a lot on a front of only half a mile. I saw poor old A. W. E. Smith, nearly bloody seventy and a carpenter, and said, "What the hell are you doing here?" and he said, "I wanted to see some of the action," and I said, "You're bloody well seeing it now," and then there was a little plop and his head fell off.

'Then there was Davidovitch, funny little fellow, a stretcher bearer. Those fellows were really kept busy, being shouted for here and there. If you could move they'd get you to get up and bloody run. I said, "You're running round like you're the local butcher saying 'Get that man on here, his leg's hanging off'" and he said, "Fred, it *is* butchery, real butchery," and so help me God as he said it his whole guts fell out like bloody giblets. It was odd. He didn't fall down, he just stood there and picked them up in his hands and stuck them back in, and there he was standing holding his bloody guts in and saying, "I've been hit, Fred, I've been hit."

'We got him on to his own stretcher and carted him back. Five of us set out to carry him and three got killed. The two of us left struggled like mad up that steep hill. I was terrified. Some people are funny in that they don't admit fear. I was then hit twice, once in the arm and elbow and once in the head, and I couldn't see for the blood pouring down my face.

'We kept meeting men and I said, "Where are the guns? There needn't be all this slaughter," and they said, "There's no ammunition." So when I got back I told George Aitken and he said what they had was the wrong ammunition anyway, and I said, "Where's the rest?" and he said, "Down there" – the fucking lorry driver was pissed and there was the lorry on its side in a ditch.

'It was evening by this time with the sun setting. I saw that bloody space, that same space those men had gone over in the morning. George went off and picked up the big, heavy, long boxes of ammunition and trudged straight across it. It was terrifying. I ran across with the boxes clutched to my stomach with some mad idea of not getting shot in the gut.

'I thought, if only we'd had support fire a whole lot of the fascists would have been dead. Anyway, we got back to the guns and loaded them and everything. There was only twelve of us in the valley and Sam Wild and his little lot of sailors. We saw the fascists streaming down the hill opposite, they were mainly Moors. I shouted, "Hold your bloody fire, if you fire now we'll all be blown to bloody eternity. If you hold your horses they won't know we're here until the morning and then you can do your stuff. The buggers won't be able to hit back and we can pick them off." One chap said, "I'll fire anyway," and I said, "If you do I'll knock your fucking head off," and I did too, just as he was going to fire.

'In the morning they came towards us and we opened up – God, you should see what Maxims can do, they dig a trench, you know. It mowed them down. Some of them had the sense to fall down as if they'd been hit, but I said to keep firing into the mob, don't stop. They lost nearly a whole bloody battalion. I was feeling really sick by then – I'd lost a lot of blood.

'We lost Kit Conroy that day, the Irish lad who was commanding No. 1 Company. He took the field just like an English gentleman going off to a hunt, saying, "Come along lads, come on now." I thought, silly bastard, and looked through my glasses. Do you know, he suddenly put a stick he was carrying on the ground, then he knelt and put his head in his hands and I thought he was praying, then I looked close through the glasses and I could see the blood

71

pouring out of him. But those guns of ours saved the Madrid–Valencia road. The Moors lost so many men they retreated, but all day we could hear our lads moaning, "Come over, we want help," but we couldn't go, we'd have been slaughtered. Some men tried to hide away. I found a number hiding underground in a wine vat.

'I remember hearing a kind of squealing and then this head bobbed over the wall. It was a boy of about sixteen, a good-looking lad. The Moors had gouged out his eyes. I can still feel that right to the bone, even after all this time. We went to help him but he died almost immediately.'

It was during this time that the battalion lost some of their Maxim guns, and there are various stories as to what happened. Fred says: 'We lost eight. Nobody knows exactly what happened. If the men with them were overtaken from the front, then whoever did it should have been seen all the time climbing up the steep slope. If that's how it happened, then they must have been bloody incompetent not to have kept a proper watch. But it's been said that a group of fascists took them in by climbing into their position singing the "Internationale", which is how they got away with it as the men were fooled. Whatever happened, the men were taken prisoner and we lost the bloody guns.

'During that day we'd about 150 of our men left in foxholes. I was told to go and get some reserve men up and talk to them about victory. I don't believe in all that fall-in-to-march-up-and-die rubbish, so I said, "I'm scared too, we're all scared, but if we stick together we've got a chance."

'We drove off a number of attacks with the remaining Maxims. I remember Sam Wild saying, "If you're frightened bloody well sing," and we sang all the time and that made them run faster than ever. Eventually I felt so bad I was told to go back and get medical treatment. On the way I met a Russian officer who told me to go back and hold the position and I said, "Don't be bloody daft, what do you think we've been doing?" There he was, all clean and tidy, in a white, spotlessly clean uniform. There was me, covered in mud and blood. Anyway, they didn't take the splinter out of my head, it's still there. The doctor said he'd bandage it up and it would correct itself, tissue would grow round it, but if he tried to dig it out serious things would happen.'

It was here Sam Wild gained his reputation of having a charmed life. He remembers his little group. 'I'd been sent out with a group I was very friendly with, felt very personally about. When we got to the position to which we'd been assigned I could see Germans and Moors massed before us. They were determined to break the position we were in. I saw the comrades I knew and loved picked off one by one until at last there was only one lad, David Brook, left on the hill with me. I'd seen the people I knew so well actually die. I don't remember now if I felt regret, remorse or even sorrow, but I knew it was frightening to know that only me and this kid was left. He was a university student, a real young lad.

'I decided that me and him couldn't win the war on us own, so we'd better pull out. So we decided to retreat in the general direction of our main battalion force. In the process I was shot at by some bloody stupid fascist with a machine gun and got four machine-gun bullets in my body. This hindered me and compelled me to lie on the floor.

'This kid picked me up and said, "I'll get you back." I said, "Sod that," and stood up. Then he got shot himself, in the leg, and was about as useful as I was. Anyway, we decided the blind can lead the blind in certain circumstances and eventually we reached the rear lines and were both shipped off to the first-aid stations. Throughout that terrible battle, though, I never thought we wouldn't win.'

Maurice Levine and Sid Quinn were, of course, there too, with the knowledge of previous campaigns behind them. Maurice, as a veteran, had been kept back and not sent into the initial attack on the first two days, but 'we lost so many men by this time, we were sent in. Almost everyone who had any position of rank had gone. The worst casualties of the war were on the Jarama and at Brunete, because in those early days the British got used as shock troops and we were so lacking in training. At least the French and Germans, if they'd not fought in the 1914–18 War, had had conscription.'

Sid had had a brief respite after Las Rozas. 'We had white bread for the first time, the most delicious meal I've ever eaten. Then we got kitted out with proper uniforms and I got a pair of boots, the best pair of boots I've ever had in my life, with wee studs in the soles – they felt like feathers. And we got silk shirts – I've always liked shirts and had a thing about silk – but we couldn't get rid of the lice as there were no proper washing facilities. The lice were as big as your finger-nails and you just transferred them.

'Anyway we didn't have much time to think about lice. We got to the Jarama and faced what seemed like a huge canvas of fire. More than a dozen boys of that original No. 1 Company were killed on the first day, we were so badly cut up. They kept being sent over the top and they got shot stone dead in minutes. They were brave men, but you can't win with bravery alone. We lost most of the officers, Winteringham himself got hit. If the German artillery had really opened up there'd have been no doubt they'd have flattened our attempts at trenches.

'Not surprisingly we got some deserters after that battle, and blokes who'd lost morale. There was a wee bit of agitation, and I remember Harry Pollitt came out and, man, were we naïve, but he moved us. What we really needed was guns, but he spoke to us, and what a speaker! The best I've bloody heard in my life. He'd bring tears to a glass eye. But the thing I remember most about the battle of the Jarama was looking down that road to Valencia and realizing there was only me and two or three other fellows holding those fascists back . . . they could have *walked* into Madrid or Valencia just like that if they'd known, it was crazy.'

Charles Morgan, the born survivor, saw 'so many lads die. Just ordinary lads. There were 101 reasons for their being out there and many, many of them were buried with their reasons.

'You're bound to get afraid under fire. Your excreta leaves you – that's normal, you lose control of the muscles if they're disturbed by fear. The man who says he's no fear –

take no notice of him. But what I saw there, and later, hardened me. I mean, we didn't take prisoners and we found some of our lads and they'd been disembowelled. We were fighting Moors, remember. They'd been led up the garden path, too, poor ignorant buggers, but good soldiers. Some were told by the Nationalists that if they wore the Christian cross bullets couldn't hurt them. The poor little bastards believed it.

'But they'd come on and on at you. I saw them mowed down by the Maxims like grass. One lad handed his gun to me, he couldn't carry on, his nerve had gone it was such a slaughter. We used old guns too, Hotchkisses, very primitive. Our equipment would have been better on exhibition in the Imperial War Museum. We wore old French helmets which wouldn't have kept a doughnut out, but they looked ornamental – the French always liked to dress their men well.

'What I remember most from that battle is using machine guns you had to urinate on to cool down. You try peeing under fire . . . but they had to be water-cooled, and that was the only way we could do it. The only thing you could do was to get down and pee on it. All hell would be breaking over your head and you'd be afraid to pull it out in case it got shot off.'

9   The Long Siege

'There's a valley in Spain called Jarama
It's a place that we all know too well,
For 'tis there that we wasted our manhood
And most of our old age as well.'
   – Charles Donnelly

In March 1937 the Republicans still held the Asturias in the north and the seaport of Santander. They also held the eastern half of the country from the Basque country in the north to just east of Málaga in the south, spreading across westwards to central Spain and Madrid, Toledo and Badajoz. The Nationalists concentrated their efforts on the beleaguered Asturias and the Basque country, while the main body of Republican forces remained dug in at Jarama. The Republicans at this time were deeply riven among themselves with bitter conflict between the communists and the POUM. During the long wait in the trenches along the Jarama river it was possible for men to have short periods of leave in Madrid, an opportunity taken eagerly by some of our volunteers. In June, the town of Bilbao fell to the Nationalists and resistance in the Basque country virtually ceased. On 17 June the British were to be pulled out of the line on the Jarama.

*

After the initial slaughter, the British Battalion settled down to a life in the trenches, interspersed with brief leave in Madrid. It was not involved in Franco's offensive in Guadalajara in March 1937.

There was still some spasmodic fighting, and, indeed, men continued to be killed or wounded during the following months, but never again, on the Jarama, in such numbers. For most of them it was to be the only lull in activities that they were to experience.

Fred Copeman came back from hospital and was made second-in-command. 'We had an excellent headquarters by that time, an old stone building, and we heaped rocks and earth on it so it stood even mortar fire. We had plenty of room – it was great. I was really proud of that headquarters.

'It was an odd kind of lull after Jarama. The battle of Guadalajara was taking place but we weren't involved. Priests used to come up and say mass for some of the lads, they were brave to do it. I found religion an amazing thing. I think it was because of my experiences in Spain that I became a Catholic later on. Some of those lads had such terrific courage – they had that something a little bit extra.

'Even though it was quiet though, from time to time the Russians would send men over the top and you could lose eighty men in an hour like that. The idea was to keep the fascist troops away from the Guadalajara front. Someone I met had been back to the Jarama recently and he said all the graves had been made into one big mound but the trenches were still there.

'Because it was slacker we could eventually let twenty-five men a day go off to Madrid for a break, and they did, and went off and got things like VD . . . The doctor gave them stuff to put on but they didn't bloody bother and in the end I said, "If you don't I'll take your trousers down before you go and the doctor'll put it on for you since you won't bother with it." They called him the cock doctor after that.

'Mind you, you couldn't really blame them. I remember when I was in hospital down on the coast. Sam Wild was there – he'd a terrible time, a burst of machine-gun fire had got him in the kidneys – and there we both were eating oranges, oranges night and day. You only had to go out and pick them. After three days I found a really badly wounded comrade crawling out of the hospital – they couldn't keep still, you know – and I said, "Here, mate, where are you going?" and he said he was looking for a brothel. "Brothel?" I told him, "If you find one you'll never get the bloody thing in." "Fred," he said, "just you leave that to me."'

Sid Quinn admits he didn't always see eye to eye with Fred Copeman as his superior officer. 'On my first leave what I did want was a nice wee drink.

'In fact, a few of us decided to have a nice wee drink of white wine. Coming from Glasgow we were not used to it and it knocked us stone out. We were staggering about all over the place. Fred had us up in front of him, and none of us was keen on that kind of discipline, and he gave us seven days. One of our lot, Tom White, tried to hit him and Fred said to him, "I'll see you when you're sober," and Tom said, "Just you wait, I'll get that bugger Copeman," but when he'd sobered up Fred fought him and he battered the daylights out of him, his nose was bust. Tom wanted to prove he was a man – no chance, Fred was a wildcat.

'Fred's penchant was for new uniforms – he was a fine-looking wee fellow in those days. He got himself purple uniforms, braided ones. It didn't detract from his efficiency as a commander, though, we'd all a great admiration for him as a soldier.

'Another time, after a trip to Madrid, we sneaked some bottles of vino back and we all had a wee drink or two. We felt very brave after that, and my mate Willy and I decided to finish the war on our own and tried to go over the top. We had to be pulled back. When I woke up the next day I'd never felt so bad in my life. Fred told us then that every time we went out we behaved like animals . . . Still, those days were soon to come to an end.'

Maurice Levine got tired of being 'wet and cold in the days of February and burnt by the sun of May and June. We were dirty and lousy and craved for sweet things like chocolate, and the smokers suffered a good deal.

'My turn arrived eventually for forty-eight hours' leave. What a delight to have a bath in a luxury hotel! It was all under the control of the Catering Workers' Union, and for a few pesetas a day my companions and I were given a suite of rooms each. Nothing was too good for the IB. Chits had to be obtained for meals in restaurants and hotels, food was scarce in Madrid. We ate at the Hotel Gran Vía. The meals were usually mule-meat and chick-peas, but the wine was excellent.

'I sat one afternoon in the café of the Gran Vía. In the centre of the floor was a huge, gilded aviary. As I looked across the quiet street on that Sunday afternoon a shell burst, killing the only two women walking along the street.

'We also rested at Mondéjar, south of Madrid. I watched the women sitting in groups shaking the bright-orange stamens of the crocus flowers for saffron and I got the kindly peasant woman to make a salad of tomatoes and onions for me dressed with olive oil and vinegar. One evening, as dusk was falling, a group of twenty peasants entered the village. Mounted on their burros, they circled the village square and their leader called out slogans.

'Waving their sickles about their heads they sang Republican songs. It was a scene I'll always remember. Our men were challenged to a game of football. The answer was apparent in the opening minutes – an overwhelming defeat for the British team.'

During the long siege of the Jarama, Charles Morgan was sent back to base for a few weeks' work, 'and it got so boring I wrote a letter to *Reynolds' News* asking readers to send out their used copies of *Reynolds'* as British newspapers were very scarce out there and got like lace curtains, they were read by so many people. About two months later a Hungarian captain arrived and shouted, "*Carole, Carole!*" He was jumping in the air and pointing. Coming down the road was a Russian camion. "For you!" he beamed. I said he was loco. "No, for you – all the mail!" No exaggeration – there were over 29,000 replies. Letters from all over the world.

'There were letters from young ladies who imagined Brigaders as kind of Beau Gestes, lean-faced men with guns and so on, proposals of marriage, fan letters from love-sick young maidens, pitiful, tragic letters from mothers whose sons had gone out to Spain and they'd heard nothing, letters from political organizations and so on. There were paperbacks by the hundred – Penguins had just started publishing – *Daily Worker*s, *Manchester Guardian*s, magazines, cigarettes, chocolates – there weren't enough censors or anybody to deal with it. However, they lent me a roneo machine and I replied to them all.'

Charles Morgan also paid a visit to Madrid and stayed at the 'posh hotel in the Gran Vía. There was no heating but beautiful bedrooms – and *sheets* . . . When we got to the reception desk the clerk said, just as calmly as if he was saying should he get us two tickets for the opera, he said would we like some girls, and he phoned up and three girls came. The only other entertainment at that time was the movie house and the only movie they had was *Modern Times*. I'd already seen it thirty-six times and I thought, if I see it again I'll scream.

'Anyway, these three girls turned up for us three comrades and said they'd go upstairs with us. One of the boys was a Romanian and he got a beautiful bird. Well, me and this girl went to bed and it was noisy because Madrid was being bombed and shelled at the time and the hotel was near the Telefónica building which they kept trying to hit. Well, there we were in bed and this girl says to me she's not very strong, no food, no strength. All the manliness and feeling of being Beau Geste came over me – I often chuckle about this now – and I said, "All right, darling, go to sleep." I don't know why I did because I was mad passionate in those days, but it would have been – I don't know – vandalism, sacrilege, but she was as thin as a lath, her poor little tits were very, very tiny. She was quite willing to go through with it, she was just telling me she was very thin.

'So I lay there and in the next room was my Romanian comrade, pumping and grunting away and me being so chivalrous.'

Garry McCartney points out the problems over girls in Spain. 'You'd see this lovely *señorita*, a real smasher, but you couldn't do much about it. I had an experience, I suppose you'd call it funny, but I found it just expensive. I used to collect savings money from the lads and pay it in for them, but suddenly they stopped paying me and said they'd all go down and pay it in themselves. I wondered what I'd done to deserve this, I was very honest, but I decided to go down and see for myself. It turned out there was a secretary there and she was really something. She'd more curves than a scenic railway.

'I just kept looking. The curves were all in the right place too. So I kept going to see her for about a week, and then I decided to pluck up courage and enough bad Spanish and ask her out for an evening. She said she'd be delighted.

'It was a Sunday evening and like all Spanish townships they start moving at about eleven o'clock at night. So there was McCartney who'd already told the lads he'd dated the Queen of Sheba and they were all down to see it. Then she arrived ready for the cinema – along with her father, her mother, her three sisters, her two brothers, and McCartney paid for them all to go in. There we sat – she was at one end of the row and I was at the other and her whole family sat in the middle. So that was my great evening out.'

However, drink and women were not the main problems arising from the long months on the Jarama. The early slaughter had frightened a number of the raw, untrained volunteers and the long wait meant that morale could drop very low, and this, as Will Paynter pointed out, has its obvious effects, one of which is desertion.

As political commissar of the XVth Brigade, George Aitken had to deal with many of these problems. Some men who wanted to go home could not be sent, however good their case, because there was just no way of replacing them and they were supposed to be committed for the duration of the war.

'But I would like to deny most vehemently what some

people have said about deserters and others being shot. In my charge were the British and Americans, and also the French, Belgians and Italians, and I can say categorically that there was nothing of the kind while I was there. I was in that job until the end of August, after the battle of Brunete, when I was called home and never got back again.

'It is true that some people higher up came and suggested it to me some time in April, on the Jarama, because it was true that some people had just taken to their heels and gone.

'The British Battalion was a cross-section of the British people, mainly the working class. There was always a corps of tremendously reliable people who were dedicated social-ists and communists, people with conviction who were there for a purpose. But there were also, of course, quite a number of people who were just out of work, and some of them had been recruited, I was told, on the Embankment.

'So there was a certain proportion that had no enthusi-asm for the war, particularly after what they had seen on the Jarama. It was not surprising as we had nothing compared to the enemy, and these lads were in the trenches for months. Anyway, some of these took to their heels and were picked up all over the place, some as far away as Barcelona. They were brought back and pushed into a house in Morata. I remember one was our quartermaster who was a man as old as me – and I was forty-two at the time – and he had done a grand job but he disappeared for a few days and then he was picked up and I went down to Morata to see him.

'He told me a story, that he'd heard from his wife and she wasn't well, and the family were hard up and so on, so he felt his duty was to get home. I felt he'd a good story, it sounded very genuine, and I remember going back to headquarters and telling Fred Copeman all about it. He'd just returned from hospital. He shouted, "Jesus Christ, George, you'll end up giving the man a medal." Anyhow, we did get him home.

'But nobody got shot. We organized them into a pioneers battalion doing various fatigues of one kind or another.

There were still those higher up, though, who wanted to try them and execute a few, and I said, "You'll do nothing of the kind while I'm here. It would be absolutely disastrous. All these men are volunteers. If ever it got back to Britain from here that you were shooting volunteers, it would be catastrophic." We were trying to recruit people. So I finally convinced them that it would be absolutely preposterous.'

On 17 June the British Battalion finally pulled out of the Jarama after seventy-three days in the line and moved back to the Albacete base. They had a bare two weeks to be able to wash, delouse and feed properly before once again they were back at the front. This was the bloody battle of Brunete.

10   Brunete

'We were freedom's foresters on that wild morning,
We trod with grace like dancers the stage of our apprehension
Waiting with gritted teeth, waiting for what would come
   out of the shadowy eaves.'
         – Jack Lindsay

After his success in the Basque country, Franco stood poised to take the Asturias. In an attempt to divert him, the Republicans launched an attack in central Spain centred on the town of Brunete to the west of Madrid. This was the first time the Republicans had initiated an attack, and to begin with it was successful. But it could not be sustained. A week after the initial attack on 13 July the offensive stage of the battle was over and the Republicans were defending the positions they had won. By the end of July the Nationalists had recaptured Brunete and Franco was poised to crush the Asturias in the north. Once he had accomplished this he could put his effort into the great push to the sea which would divide the Republic in two. By the time the Republicans had taken stock in the aftermath of Brunete, the war in the north was lost.

*

It was in July that the Republic went into the offensive, and the choice was Brunete, to the north of the Madrid–El Escorial road. The idea was to try and cut off the besieging

Nationalist forces around Madrid from the west. The Republicans hoped to achieve this aim before Franco, who had been fighting in the Basque country, could send reinforcements.

The XVth Brigade, which was now under the command of Čopíc, was to be used as a shock force. The initial attack was extremely successful, but all was to become confusion and opinion is divided to this day over the strategic planning of the operation. Some of those involved, as we shall see, still feel bitter about it.

The battle raged around the villages of the Castilian plain. Both sides suffered from thirst in the terrific heat but again, the Nationalists showed the superiority of their armaments. They were aided at Brunete, for the first time, by Messerschmitt fighters.

Fighting continued until almost the end of July by which time the Nationalists had recaptured Brunete itself. The losses of the International Brigades were dreadful. The Lincoln and Washington Battalions lost so many men that they had to be merged and the British Battalion endured similar slaughter. The fiercest battles were fought between 9 and 18 July in the struggle for what came to be known as 'Mosquito Hill', the key to the heights of Romanillos.

The communist George Brown died at Brunete. Charles Donnelly, who had written the famous song of the Jarama battle, died too, and many, many more.

More than any other action, Brunete divides those who took part in it. The battle was fought over a wide area around many little villages and obviously any one participant saw only his part of the battlefield. To Sid Quinn it was totally mismanaged, but Charlie Morgan found the attack well organized. All the participants were shaken by the ferocity of the response. The battalion lost the remarkable and controversial George Nathan at Brunete, and George Aitken saw him buried under highly dramatic circumstances. It would seem, too, that if it had not been for George Aitken the British losses at Brunete would have been even higher than they were, which gives even more value to his account, which closes the chapter.

Sid Quinn takes up the story. 'We knew soon after we'd been withdrawn from the Jarama that we were going off to take Brunete. This was a different kettle of fish altogether. We had more troops than ever before and we had had a good many replacements for those we lost on the Jarama. We thought this had to be the end of the bloody war. We arrived at the front after an overnight march. We were to attack the village of Villanueva de la Cañada.

'As we moved down our aircraft came over, and you should have seen what we had . . . some of them were old tri-planes. They were weaving about the sky like dodgems and they got shot down like pheasants. Those poor buggers up there – they were sitting in undertakers' traps, very few got away. You can imagine what we felt about the non-interventionist powers and their refusal to supply the Re-public when it was in such desperate straits.

'Our first objective was to take the village of Villanueva de la Cañada. If Franco's troops knew nothing else, they knew how to fortify – every position was a killer. The Dimi-trovs tried to storm it and lost fifty men, and then we tried it and couldn't get through the wire. Copeman, who was com-manding the battalion, said to try and go round and do it from the other side but not to stay lying out in the open. Franco had Krupp quick-firing guns which were very ef-ficient.

'The sun was beating down. God, it was warm! We were really thirsty. We had already taken a lot of casualties – Maurice Levine got shot up then. I didn't see what hap-pened. I suddenly got a call of nature and had to go over this wee culvert, which I did, and when I came back Maurice had gone. Fred, with his staff round him, was sheltering by the culvert and I remember one wee lad of seventeen, whose arm was shattered and he didn't make a sound, he just stood there holding it. My friend Jones from Belfast was there. I saw him lying down shot through the mouth and could do nothing about it. He was quite phlegmatic about it, he knew it was no good, so I just turned him over to make him more comfortable and he died.

'Well, we took that village in the end, but we took it twelve hours too late. There I saw the worst incident of the war. A group of civilians were pushed out of the village towards the end of the fighting, mostly women and children. We wondered what was happening until we saw they were being used as a living shield, they were screaming. It was ghastly to watch it. There were old men, babies, toddlers, and they were shot down by us because we couldn't stop. Every last one of them.

'It all became a shambles. We should have carried on with the offensive, carried on across country. We should never have stayed where we were. We could have left a holding party of troops and taken Brunete in strength and then gone on from there. What persuaded the command to take the line they did I don't know.

'There we were in trouble again with no artillery coming up to support us. But we advanced for a further two days to Mosquito Hill and we were shelled all the way. I remember seeing four bulls grazing quietly on the hill under all the shot and shell until they tumbled and fell over with their legs up. It was tragic to see poor innocent beasts killed like that.

'Our casualties were awful. Charlie Goodfellow had his head blown off as he lay wounded in Copeman's arms. We didn't have time to bury them, we just had to keep moving. I remember when the shelling was getting us down seeing Clifford Wattis, the actor's brother, who looked a real English aristocrat, all peaches and cream, sitting down and *shaving* in a wee mirror without taking elementary precautions. It cheered us all up to think of what that wee chap was doing in the middle of that fascist onslaught. He had a charmed life and he didn't get wounded until right at the end of the war.

'Franco threw everything up in his counter-attack. It took three days to even get any rations to us. Albert Charlesworth walked miles to try and get food to us. We stayed on Mosquito Hill with hardly any food or water. Then we had a really bizarre happening – only the communists could do it. We were told Frank Pitcairn was going to speak to us, he would hold a meeting. A meeting! We were under a perfect barrage of artillery and snipers when Pitcairn came up in a van, driven by a driver who had got wounded on the way. His lady friend had been killed on the way up, too.

'He told us Eden was going to drop his non-intervention policy. The stupidity of it, the awful stupidity. He wasn't even right in what he said, and there we were holding a meeting under shell-fire. Sixteen men were *killed* at that meeting, the snipers just picked them off one after the other.

'There was another frightful incident at this point. We saw a Spanish boys' battalion going into the fight – their average age was fourteen, I should guess. I don't know who gave the order, but Franco just wiped them out, cut them to ribbons. We could hear the screams of those boys dying for hours. They lay out in the hot sun of the day and the cold night that followed, screaming and sobbing, and we couldn't go over and lose even more men so we had to sacrifice those boys. One of our men did volunteer and go and see what he could do, but he immediately got shot.

'The slaughter just went on. Bob Elliot of Newcastle dropped dead beside me, some of my good Irish friends died there. It was a tragic waste of life. There was no relief. Poor Copeman, he soon had only fifty men left. It was a massive blunder to allow such losses. As they continued he weighed up the situation and decided to take us back although we lost more men even doing that.

'We had to leave our wounded where they were. We left men with their stomachs lying out trying to hold them in, we couldn't carry them. There were entrails lying around all over the place from those brave men. When we got back from the hill we found that Nathan had been killed.

'I'd like to know who was behind those military tactics, whose stupid idea it was to go on and on trying to take one village instead of leaving a holding force there and carrying on and making use of the valuable time. The men did Herculean work, but it was at that point in the game that I knew the war was lost in Spain.'

His close friend, Maurice Levine, who had been right through the war with him, saw little of Brunete. 'I was nearly killed before I even got there. The truck I was in jolted into a ditch throwing some of us out. The rear wheel passed over one man, killing him. He was a miner from Durham who had shown me how to swing a pick on the Jarama when we dug trenches.

'For days the temperature had topped 100 degrees, we were frantic for water. We dug in the dried-up bed of a river to find foul-smelling water a couple of feet below. It was vile, but we drank it and some of us were sick.

'But I saw little more. Probably I was lucky to be wounded on that first day outside Villanueva de la Cañada as 300 of us went into action and twenty days later only forty-five remained.'

It was to be the end of the road for Charlie Morgan too. 'I'd been back working at base, but I persuaded them to send me back to the battalion. The men were marching off to war, it was like a film. Actually I thought the Brunete battle was, at least at first, very well organized. It was the first time the brigade had actually been on the offensive as opposed to the defensive. It was well planned, they'd learned something.

'I'll always remember what it looked like on that first day. It was like a panorama. It's hard to describe Spain, your vision is so wonderful. With the clarity of the atmosphere you can see villages five or six miles away, you don't get mist like in England. The view from the top of that hill . . . you could see everything going on just as if it was a big set for a Hollywood movie. We were plagued by locusts as big as your fists – we used to crack 'em.

'I was with a machine-gun unit when we were told to go over the top. I remember this lovely lad – I send a pound a year to the *Morning Star* as a memorial to him – turning to me and grinning, and he said, "Eeh, Charlie, it's like being in the pictures, isn't it." That was it. He was killed. I saw most of the rest of the battle, but it gets increasingly difficult to remember, and then I can't remember any more.'

Fred Copeman remembers all too vividly the assault on Mosquito Hill which he had to lead. 'It was a steep hill, a bloody awful climb for the men, but if we'd stopped it would have been fatal. You had to force the men to climb a bloody mountain after walking for hours in the sun. When we got there and I looked back, my Christ, we were in an impossible bloody position. There was nothing to hide behind, it was a real death-trap. Their planes were coming over so low you could almost see the pilot's eyes. We looked across at the Washington Battalion. Suddenly there was a bang and a huge pile of smoke and there were only thirty-two of them left – they were massacred in seconds.

'I thought the only sensible thing was to get the hell out of it. We'd problems with grub. They'd try and send us food up from headquarters and the machine guns would get them every time. Some people do things you can't explain. This lad made it his job to get our food up if he could, and he did it under the most terrible conditions. Then he tried it by night to see if it was easier, and the searchlights got him, and they had him in the end, shot him down. He was such a kid and he'd been so brave some of the lads thought we should bury him.

'We dug a hole quietly – very shallow, only about two feet – we crawled out and got him by the legs. At this moment the silly little bugger hit a rock, which was good timing as the shot landed where we would have been. Then it hit his body again and we were covered with this awful, purple, mass of pulp and this terrible stink.

'We'd managed to hold that awful bloody position, but it was no good. We were just stuck out on a limb, so I thought we had to get out. Sam Wild had got it again. He and Bob Elliott were arguing over something and two bullets went through one after the other, they killed two people including Bob, and one went through Sam's thigh. God, Sam was a good lad, a brave lad.

'The attack went wrong. After taking Brunete we should have pushed straight on, we should never have wasted all that time and those lives as we did by concentrating on

90

taking those small villages. Eventually we did get orders to pull out, and it was just as well. I was worried sick by this time with visions of us all being completely wiped out.'

Sam Wild, as Copeman says, was wounded at Brunete before his wounds had properly healed from the Jarama. So many officers were killed at Brunete that he had been given command of all the infantry left, some ninety men, and joined Copeman on the assault on Mosquito Hill. 'Why did we call it that? Because the bullets came off it like mosquitos.'

The British, in their attempt to take the hill, succeeded against all odds in taking ridge after ridge on the way up. But they never took the fortified top, and it was the hours of fighting from a weak position, while being raked with fire from the top, that claimed such heavy casualties.

It might be that, without the efforts of George Aitken, these would have been even worse.

'There's so much one could say about Brunete, too much. To begin with, during that battle we lost one of the great figures of the whole war – George Nathan, that mysterious man, East End Jew, guardsman, always immaculate, always carrying his cane. He'd been attached to the brigade staff on the Jarama under Gal, but they didn't get on and towards the end of the time there he'd been working with the French XIVth Brigade. However, he returned in time for Brunete.

'He was made chief of operations for the brigade and was in the thick of it right through until towards the end of the battle. The British hadn't had a day out. We stood side by side looking across a field, and suddenly all we could see was new Spanish troops walking away from the battle.

'Nathan was out there with his stick, whacking them on the bottom and getting them to turn round. We did this for an hour or two and got a considerable number to go back. Finally it slackened off a bit and he said he'd go back and see how the transport was getting on, and I said I'd see how the British were faring. There was only a small number left – about fifty or sixty of the hundreds that went into battle. There they were, lying about almost dead from fatigue, between the heat, thirst and lack of food. I wasn't there very long when a flight of planes came over and I took cover, shortly after which I heard Nathan had been hit. He'd gone over to see the transport and, as usual, as he felt he had a charmed life, he didn't take cover and bombs fell and he was hit badly and carried away.

'Shortly after an order came from the division that the brigade had to go back into the line, the new troops had broken again and the line was folding up. It was bloody terrible. How could they go back, fifty or sixty British and the other battalions who, although they hadn't been so badly hammered as us, had had a bad time? In fact the XIVth Brigade, the French, were so shot up that when they got the order to march they turned round and marched the other way.

'So I said to the acting brigade commander, the original one had been wounded, "this is preposterous, it's impossible, you know the state the troops are in". So we took it up with the division, with Gal, and he just said, "It's an order." So I said to the brigade commander, a German, "I don't think we should put up with this. We should appeal over his head to the corps commander."

'So I persuaded him we'd go and look for the corps headquarters as we didn't know where it was. After an hour we located them and we arrived and told the officers there what our business was. They said, "This isn't done. You can't approach the corps commander over the head of the division. It isn't etiquette"; and the other man, who'd been an officer in the German army, saw the point and said okay, he wouldn't press it. I said, "You can do what the bloody hell you like, but I'm damn well insisting I get in to see the corps commander. I think it's madness to order our people back into action." They could hardly drag themselves along the road.

'They took me into a big room, the usual thing, slightly darkened to keep out the sun. I saluted and so on and told my story about the condition of the troops and that this was an impossible order.

'I saw my people were in no condition to fight, they were already half-dead. The corps commander looked at me across the table and said quietly, "We may all be dead before nightfall." That rocked me back on my heels. So I said to him, "If that's the case, there's nothing more to be said," and I saluted and went out. There *was* nothing more to be said. If the whole thing was so desperate that the front was folding up – as happened later on the Ebro – that was it. So I went back and gave the news to the battalion.

'Copeman had collapsed and Wally Tapsell and Jock Cunningham paraded the few remaining men and said this was the position and we had to go back in, when suddenly an order came. The corps must have been in touch with the division and a new order was sent saying they didn't have to go. The front had stabilized. Perhaps it had, but I like to think that maybe my insistence had had some effect.

'Why had they been so hard hit? It was partly the way the battle went and partly how they'd been placed.

'The next thing we heard was that Nathan had died in hospital. Because of what he had been to us, they decided to bury him in state. They rigged him up in a box and they brought him down to Brunete in the evening. We couldn't bury him by day because the planes were coming over. Most of the leading people came from the brigade, including Gal, although he and Nathan had quarrelled most bitterly. Cunningham was there too, although he had also had a few problems with Nathan.

'Anyway, at darkness we dug a hole and put the body in, and I gave a short funeral oration about his legendary virtues and so on, and while I'm talking – and by this time it was practically dark apart from a cold moon – I could hear both General Gal and Cunningham sobbing. Both of them were feeling the fact that they hadn't been on terms with this great soldier.

'It reminded me of that poem about the burial of Sir John Moor at Corunna – "Not a drum was heard nor a funeral note." Slowly and slowly we laid him down. Poor Nathan

. . . he'd been so long at the front he thought he'd a charmed life. Mind you, so did I. Cunningham did too until towards the end of his time on the Jarama. There was a hullabaloo up the trench somewhere and Copeman went off to do something about it and Cunningham jumped over the trench and got hit in the belly and the arm, I think. After that, at Brunete, he and I were going across a very big field and I was walking straight to the other side. But Cunningham said, "No, don't make a beeline like that, keep well down and go right round the perimeter." He wouldn't have done that before he got wounded.

'My luck continued to hold, though. All I got was a slight hit from some shrapnel – I was never out of action.'

11 Welcomes and Farewells

Brunete, in a number of ways, became a turning point. It did delay Franco's attack on the Asturias, but did not prevent the eventual outcome. The Republicans gained a small amount of ground in central Spain, but at enormous cost, including the loss of their air superiority. After Brunete the British Battalion had to pick up its shattered remnants and count its punitive losses. Many men had died and even more had been wounded and had to be sent home. It was a period of changeover, with many of the early volunteers being invalided back to Britain to be replaced by new blood fresh from basic training at Albacete.

*

Brunete, as we have seen, brutally reduced the British Battalion. How did the men feel afterwards, those who had survived and seen so many comrades killed or wounded? Sid Quinn spoke for the lads from Scotland who were with him when he said: 'It got so bad in the end, all you could think was that you were glad it wasn't you . . . You couldn't go back for them, you couldn't do anything.

'It's no good dwelling on what went wrong and the men who died – they're dead. But as I said, it was after Brunete I decided the war was hopeless. I was asked if I'd like to go on leave and do some propaganda work at home and I decided I'd go. There were hardly any of us left from that original party which fought at Lopera. It was very disconcerting when people kept saying to me, "My God, are you still

95

alive?" I didn't think my luck would hold out.

'Anyway, I decided to work elsewhere. The fellow on the ground sees all the mistakes and he pays for them with his life. The high-ups pay for them with their reputations.'

Maurice Levine had no option but to go home as he had been badly hurt. 'I'd been wounded in the first fascist sortie out of Villanueva de la Cañada, and all that afternoon and evening I lay out in the fields between Quijorna and Villanueva. I'd had a slighter wound at Jarama, and by a weird coincidence the same two Americans who were at the advanced field station at Brunete also looked after me at Jarama. "I'll be doggone," said one when they saw me carried in. "It's that bugger Levine again!" They gave me a shot of morphine and I was sick, perhaps from the stagnant, foul water I'd been drinking that day. The whole area seemed to me to be ablaze, but the morphine took effect and I fell asleep.

'The next morning I was moved to the rear. I asked the Spanish doctors whether my arm was broken as it felt useless. "*Carne*," he replied. A flesh wound, that was all, but my bicep had been damaged by a bullet. I was then moved to an enormous place – San Lorenzo del Escorial. Here the rooms were all used for the severely wounded and the dying. From there I went to Madrid. That hospital was most unpleasant – Velázquez 62. It was alleged that the medical staff were secret fascist supporters. André Diamond, the gallant French Jew who had fought with the British since Lopera, had his leg amputated there, and he thought it could have been saved. Poor André, when the Nazis entered Paris he was betrayed to the Gestapo and executed.

'I was actually in hospital quite a long time. I was bandaged up finally in Madrid with an aeroplane splint. It was a type of dressing for that kind of wound that they used in the First World War. It was wildly out of date, but the Spanish doctors didn't know that.

'It fastened my arm tight to my body because, with my bicep being damaged, they didn't want me to use my arm. Finally, when they did take the dressing off, my arm was quite rigid, it wouldn't move, and I remembered seeing men from the First War who had had similar types of wound. When our doctor, Tudor Hart, saw it he said if it didn't show any signs of movement within a week he'd have to operate, break it, and try and do something about it again.

'Luckily, a day or two later I helped out a man loading some timber, in spite of my bad arm. He wasn't a member of the battalion, he was an ambulance driver and his name was George Green. (He was the husband of Nan, who is now the secretary of the International Brigade Association.) Anyway, he helped me pick up pieces of wood with my hand, and gradually I found I could move my arm more and more so that eventually I got most of the use back. Then, after a time in an American convalescence centre, I was sent home.'

Charles Morgan convalesced at Valencia, 'Then I was shipped up to Barcelona and I reached England in a very peculiar way. I was put on an English boat, and do you know what its cargo had been? Guano – bird shit! It was used as a fertilizer and it showed how optimistic the Republic was, shipping in fertilizer. Anyway, I stank by the time I got home.'

Fred Copeman and George Aitken were recalled to Britain along with some other veterans from the early days, Jock Cunningham and Wally Tapsell. Tapsell was a controversial figure throughout the war, but he went back. Jock Cunningham and George Aitken, due to internal conflicts within the British Communist Party, were not allowed to return.

It still goes deep with George Aitken and it appears to have destroyed Jock Cunningham. Fred Copeman says: 'Poor, bloody man. Why they treated him as they did I'll never know. Happily, the attitude of the party has changed a lot since then, that awful virtuous political attitude to other peoples' views has gone and it's all more humane now. But he never recovered from it and he died a bloody tramp, picking up fag-ends. No one knew when he died, no one cried for him. He'd a pauper's bloody funeral. He deserved better.'

Bob Cooney, whose time did not overlap with Cunningham's, came across him in sad circumstances many years later. 'Jock was an elemental person in every sense of the word. He read and read and read, anything and without discrimination. He'd had such acclaim at first, and then when he fell out with the party it affected his mind. He fell on bad times in the end and I' remember somebody late in 1938 or 1939 trying to get him a job because of his past reputation, but he was already hitting the roads by that time and couldn't settle down. One day he just walked off into the blue again. Later, much later, in 1951 I was speaking in the Market Place at Aberdeen and someone said, "There's an old comrade over there."

'It was Jock Cunningham. He said to me, "Still in the political game, are you? You're wasting your time, the only way you'll change the world is by getting into peoples' minds." He'd been in and out of asylums for the past seven years and he was dossing in a cheap lodging house in Aberdeen. He had been a hero – especially at Jarama – but I think they had tried to make an image of him that he couldn't live up to, and that's what went wrong. They tried to make him an intellectual, too. He had a quick mind, and perhaps he would have been one eventually, but they tried too quick – you have to start with the soup course . . . Nobody knows when or where he died.'

George Aitken still does not enjoy going into his differences to this day, but after endless fruitless arguments and bitter discussions the party decided he should not return to Spain no matter how strong his protests. In one way perhaps it was fortunate as he survived the war, but because of the political disagreement, the Communist Party in Britain deprived the British Battalion of not only a fine soldier but of one of the most brilliant administrators within its ranks.

The few remnants of the British Battalion were reconstituted, and during the autumn and early winter of 1937 they were joined by more volunteers from Britain. It was after Brunete that Joe Norman begged the party to send him out to Spain. 'We went first to the old fortress of Figueras, and then after a few days we were passed on from there to a training base at Tarazona. After three weeks' training we joined the British Battalion in September 1937 and were told things were fairly quiet.

'We newcomers were not to know that the action for the newly organized British Battalion was about to start and would continue, non-stop, until after the battle of Teruel in the early part of 1938. It was in that September, too, that the Republican government incorporated the International Brigades into the Spanish Republican army and they became subject to a more conventional form of army discipline. The men had to spend their time digging trenches and generally training themselves for mountain warfare.

'It wasn't all grim. Wally Tapsell, who was back by that time, organized a sports festival, and boxing events were held in a bull ring. I knocked out the Indian Army champion – poor chap was killed later at Teruel – and I also fought the American "Golden Gloves" champion and beat him easily, although by that time I only weighed ten stone and he weighed fourteen. We had all kinds of visitors, too, Clement Attlee, Noel Baker, J. B. S. Haldane, Harry Pollitt. The No. 1 Company of the British Battalion got called after Attlee as a result of his visit.

'During the dinner for Harry Pollitt I decided to sing a folk song from Russia, "Stenka Razin". Nobody wanted to hear it, but Harry insisted I could if I wanted to, everybody has a democratic right to sing . . .'

Bill Feeley from St Helens arrived about the same time as Joe, 'and I was really lucky. I got more training than most in Spain as I was sent to a sniping school. We had some people teach us how to use rifles, new Russian ones. The school was in a pinewood and our days seemed pretty long. The instructor was a Russian and he did his best to make soldiers out of us.

'He said the British were the worst of all. The Germans marched dead regimental-like and sung in unison. The Slavs sung best, they used to sing in perfect harmony with their sergeant walking in front of them beating time. But whatever that Russian said, the British were the best marksmen. We were given new uniforms while we were there, but they were so fragile that if you lay on the ground to shoot you broke all the seams.

'You also got in friendly arguments with other folk on politics. Most people who are political have their own way of expressing things – a kind of jargon, I suppose – and a lot the communists said sounded queer to people like me. Anyway, they taught me the words of "The Red Flag" and the "Internationale" as I didn't even know them. I thought the English words were proper queer at the time.

'The food was diabolical. The rationing we'd had in the Great War was nothing on it. You'd have to have a permit for a meal, get in a queue, but if you told people you were in the IB, they'd often let you go to the front. We dreamed of food. Some chaps'd come over from America in the *Queen Mary* and they showed us their luxury menus as we tried not to pull faces over soup with garlic and awful thick oil floating on the top of bean stew. But you got used to it after a while – and the wine. I'd drink all the newcomers' wine rations, too, drink was drink and food was food. I remember once falling asleep after a lot of wine with me mouth open, and when I woke up it were full of dead flies – full.

'I tried learning a bit of Spanish before going off to fight. The Spaniards used to laugh uproariously at it. We were lazy about learning it, I suppose, but those of us like me – who just *have* to talk – learnt a bit. However, all the different battalions learnt to communicate with each other in elementary Spanish. I used to sing "La Paloma" as a duet with a big Spanish sergeant.

'All the time, though, local people were very friendly. I remember an old man taking me to his house and showing me his two fat daughters and asking me which one I'd like to marry. Then there were the flamenco competitions. They would vie with each other how many variations they could get into that final note. It were like a cup tie at the end, with all the supporters shouting and screaming, "*Olé, Olé!*"'

100

12   Teruel

During the period in which the Nationalist forces were beating down the last resistance in the north, the Republicans had some small success with diversionary attacks in the Aragón. They took the town of Belchite and dug in there. But the news from the north could only prove disheartening. By taking the Asturias, Franco had gained the Republicans' rich coalfields and much heavy industry. Again there was a brief lull in hostilities. Towards the end of 1937, Franco decided to try again for Madrid, but his plans were discovered by the Republicans, who launched another diversionary attack, again in the Aragón. The place they chose was Teruel, and it was hoped that they would both divert Franco from his push for Madrid and assist their own communications with the northern part of the province.

*

Teruel is the austere, walled capital of a province known for its poverty and the fact that in winter it records the lowest temperatures in the whole of Spain. It is celebrated, says Hugh Thomas, 'for the glum legend of the *Lovers of Teruel*, which often attracts those who desire a melancholy theme for a short ballet. This gloomy history was a suitable background for the atrocious battle of Teruel, which lasted for over two months.'

The Republican attack began on 15 December, in driving snow and without aerial or artillery support as it was considered that this way there would be more chance of a surprise attack. The attack did, in fact, surprise Franco, but he quickly determined to mount a massive counter-attack.

Over Christmas the Republicans besieged Teruel, and by 29 December they were themselves under attack from the Nationalist forces. The weather was appalling, with three feet of snow and temperatures registering 18° below zero. Both armies got cut off from their supply routes and hundreds of vehicles had to be abandoned in drifts of snow.

The men who had survived Brunete's blazing heat and the hard terrain of the Aragón in the autumn found themselves fighting frostbite at Teruel in the winter. In early January the Republicans took Teruel, but gradually they found themselves in the position of the besieged instead of the besiegers. A Nationalist attack on 7 February meant a loss to the Republic of 7,000 prisoners and 15,000 casualties, along with a vast amount of equipment, munitions, arms and ambulances. They also lost 500 square miles of ground.

The last battle took place on 20 February and the Republicans were forced to continue their retreat. They managed to pull out the majority of their troops, but again they left behind badly needed arms and equipment and a substantial number of prisoners.

The initial fighting at Teruel had been undertaken largely by the Spanish troops with the International Brigades held in reserve, and it was in mid-January that the British, along with the Canadians, saw front line action as they attempted to halt a Spanish advance down the valley leading directly into Teruel. The battalion was posted on a high cliff overlooking the valley.

Most British casualties occurred when the battalion tried to stem a Nationalist attack coming down the valley and found themselves caught between the Nationalist advance and the covering fire of their own machine guns on the heights above. But it was to no avail, and by mid-February the British Battalion had pulled out with the rest. Apart from the crossing of the Ebro in the summer of 1938, the battalion, however bravely it fought, would now be fighting in the rearguard actions of a retreating army.

British accounts of what happened at Teruel are sketchy. Most of the experienced men had gone after Brunete, and those who fought at Teruel were flung straight in at the deep end and did not know what to expect. They were unaware of the strategy behind the battle and were suffering from the intense cold. To the British it was incredibly confusing. They were thrown into the thick of the action, withdrawn and sent away from the front and then immediately told to return to it. By the time they returned the battle was over and lost. Their accounts can only be peripheral.

It was at Teruel, says Garry McCartney and some of the other volunteers from Glasgow, that 'you began to realize the massive difference in strength between the two armies. It was to get more apparent as time went by, but it was really noticeable at Teruel, they could bring up more and more men.'

Fred Copeman had returned from sick leave shortly before the Teruel offensive, bringing with him something of a superstition. 'I'd got hold of this pair of cavalry boots, absolutely smashing they were, really posh, but for some reason they weren't all that comfortable and I didn't wear them. Then a Russian borrowed them, and there he was in a silver and blue uniform, right in the front line, a uniform that shouted "Shoot me – I'm the one" and not surprisingly he got killed. The boots were returned to me.

'I had them a few days and then some bloke pinched them –and would you believe, he got killed. They came back to me again. A mate of mine was about to be repatriated and he asked if he could borrow the boots and he did. I said to him, "With those boots, it's lucky you're going home to-morrow," and there was a loud bang, and blow me, his head had gone. I carried them around with me after that as a kind of charm, but I told everybody, "For God's sake, don't wear them!"

'Anyway I got to Teruel all set for action when I got a pain in my stomach. It got so bad they said they'd take me to hospital, and I said I can't go into hospital *now*, but they did anyhow, as it seems I was seriously ill. Bill Alexander took over, with Sam Wild as his adjutant. Anyway, off I went to hospital in an ambulance they called "the love wagon" because it had a *gorgeous* nurse in it and they found I had a gangrenous appendix. The operation was serious and took three hours – it was a bad thing to have in those days.

'I came round and it looked as if I'd soon be better and I was itching to get up and go back to the front, then one day, when they must have been in the thick of it at Teruel, I somehow couldn't see and I thought someone was sitting on my chest. I managed to call out, "Do something, I think I'm dying," and everybody belted in, and there I was croaking my head off. I'd had a relapse and I nearly did die. I woke up later with bottles of saline and blood and tubes and so on attached to me, but after that I gradually got better.'

The most experienced leaders left were Bill Alexander and Sam Wild. The indefatigable Sam had returned to the front after recovering from his wound at Brunete.

For most of the battalion, as it was now formed, Teruel was their first engagement, and it was a baptism of fire in every sense of the word, with many men being killed – thirteen in the Major Attlee Company alone.

'Fighting itself?' says Bob Cooney. 'At first we looked forward to it. Volunteers spend so much of their time marching around and getting buggered about that you keep thinking when are you going to get on with it, let's do what we've come for.

'When it got to it, at Teruel, people reacted to the actual fighting in different ways. Some were more scared than others – it wasn't their fault, it's the way you're made, although I think most soldiers are the same. There you are, waiting for something to relieve the boredom – the soldier's worst enemy is boredom, hanging around aimlessly. Then you go into action and you wonder how you'll feel physically. Will you be frightened? Will the other lads know you're frightened? I was most frightened by my own gun when they put me on a machine gun. I was frightened of what I was dishing out myself.'

Bob Cooney had arrived, complete with his own difficult reputation, and 'also I was told that Aberdonians had a reputation for being a dour lot. I was first of all put on producing the newspaper *Volunteer for Liberty* which I used to take up to Teruel before the action started. But I didn't get on very well with my superiors. They said I suffered from "rank and filist tendencies". Anyway, for these tendencies I was demoted to *soldado* and I ended up in the trenches at Teruel. Copeman had become ill and Bill Alexander was to take his place, and then *he* got wounded.

'Sam did some clever diversionary work, attacking down a valley at Teruel, and he inflicted quite a bit of damage. It was a long and hard battle, Teruel, and so cold, so cold. I remember crawling into a ravine to get water for the overheated machine guns, and the artillery fire kept on incessantly over this ravine. It gave you a really uneasy sensation in your neck and spine as you tried to break the ice and then melt it into water and cool the guns with it. It was a terrible struggle. Then you did what you could with a rifle.

'There was a lot of firepower directed at us. After the fascist advance it became murderous throughout that long battle. We were pulled out at one stage and promised a rest, and we went down the road and I actually slept in the Duke of Alba's bed – then we were suddenly called back. The front had fallen, Teruel had been retaken. I think during that action we were all afraid – the important thing was not to communicate your fear.'

Eddie Brown from Glasgow remembers the brief respite at Teruel too. 'We'd been there in the freezing cold for six weeks and we were told we'd have a break. We went by train or bus to Valencia, and we were so relieved to be getting out. Then, as soon as we got there, we were told we had to get back and we had to just turn round and go. Some of those in the buses had just got off when they found the people who had arrived in front of them telling them to get straight back, the front had collapsed or something. They rounded everybody up to go back, and I remember men going into action that night wearing all kinds of things, some of them half-shaved and so on.'

It was after Teruel that Sam Wild became commander of the British Battalion. He had done brilliant work at Teruel. 'Teruel was tragic,' he says. 'It began as a major victory for the Republic and ended as a major defeat.'

13   The Long Defeat

'The stars are dead; the animals will not look:
We are left alone with the day and the time is short and
*   History to the defeated*
May say Alas but cannot help or pardon.'
*   – W. H. Auden, 'Spain 1937'*

In February 1938, Franco launched a counter-attack in the Aragón. The Republicans withdrew with massive losses, not only of men but also of vital equipment. It was apparent by this time that the Nationalist forces were vastly superior in men and armaments. The fighting was accompanied by heavy bombing on Barcelona in the north. In March the Republicans received slight encouragement from a victory at sea when a Republican naval force, led by the cruiser *Libertad*, sank the Nationalist cruiser *Baleares*. But Franco followed up his success in the Aragón with a second offensive in March, taking Belchite, Caspe, Lérida and Gandesa. In the north, the Nationalist advance continued into Catalonia, and on 3 April they achieved their biggest objective. A force under General Antonio Aranda reached the Mediterranean at Vinaroz and cut Republican Spain in two.

*

A month after the fall of Teruel, the British Battalion and the International Brigades fought in a minor action at

Segura de los Banos, a hundred miles north of Teruel. They successfully halted a Nationalist advance, and the commander of the British Battalion, Bill Alexander, and his adjutant, Sam Wild, distinguished themselves in action.

Alexander took half the battalion and pushed to the head of the valley from which the brigades had taken up their position and pushed back a Nationalist attack, supported by the fire of the second half of the battalion from the top of the hill. In the action, however, he was wounded. Sam Wild said: 'I was conducting my own operation when I saw that Bill had fallen with a wound in his arm. He shouted across, "I'm wounded, Sam, I leave you in charge." I told him okay and to go off and get a clean bill of health, all a bit silly like.'

Unfortunately, complications set in and Alexander did not return. Sam Wild became commander of the battalion until it was withdrawn. 'I took over, in fact, command of all the English-speaking forces. I enjoyed it, I loved it – telling the Yanks what to do and when to do it.'

But the brigades were soon to be rushed back to the Aragón. On 8 March, Franco launched a massive offensive in the Aragón and the front collapsed. What followed was a headlong retreat until the frontiers of Catalonia were reached and a new line established between the rivers Ebro and Segre.

Once again the British found themselves at Belchite, but this time fighting an abortive rearguard action. They fought at Belchite, at Caspe, and suffered many casualties in the bitter defence of Gandesa. At Belchite they were under bombardment from heavy machine-gun and artillery fire, and from the air until they were literally blown out. When the order came to retreat they covered the road, and the battalion was the last to leave the town, having held off the Nationalist advance for a day and enabled a sizeable number of troops to get away.

In the early hours of 10 March they linked up with the Americans and Spanish, who had been making a fighting retreat for thirty-six hours and were exhausted. The eleventh of March found the battalion practically encircled, and only a silent forced march enabled them to escape. On 12 March they reached brigade headquarters at Vinaceite, but the line was still in full retreat and they were told to fall back to Hijar.

They then retreated to Caspe and prepared for a long siege; men were rushed across country, machine guns lashed to tanks, new recruits rushed without experience from the Albacete base. The progress towards Caspe could be clearly seen from the air: a trail of dead men, lost equipment and burnt-out vehicles. British casualties were heavy as they fought a rearguard action at Caspe on 15 March; there was no long siege. Caspe proved a death trap, and again the battalion and the International Brigades were almost encircled.

The offensive halted on 17 March and the exhausted troops had about ten days' respite, but on 30 March the Nationalists struck again, this time at Gandesa. Although resistance from the Republicans was stiff and better organized, it availed little. One group of Britons who were defending a hill managed to get away in the dark, but others were overtaken by the speed of the fascist advance. On 31 March one of the war's veterans, Wally Tapsell, was killed. The remnants of the XVth Brigade managed to hold up the fascist advance for nearly twenty-four hours at Gandesa to allow the main force to pull out. By the beginning of April the retreat had become a rout, and on 15 April the Nationalist forces finally reached the sea and cut Spain in two.

The stories of the men involved in the collapse of the Aragón front are those of men swept away in a defeat which was to become a rout. It was every man for himself. A few survived to fight in the last battles of the war. Others were to serve out their time as prisoners-of-war. Their feelings, with only a few exceptions, become those of men forced into realizing that their dream would not come true. The Republican cause was lost.

Bob Doyle joined the battalion at Belchite. 'We'd been training with wooden rifles at Albacete ... I heard there was a rumour that there was to be a draft up to the front and three lorries were going, so I just jumped on one. I decided to go anyway, without asking anybody's permission. So that's how I ended up at Belchite. I got into trouble for going there without permission, got a reprimand, but they were desperate for people with experience, so I was put in charge of a machine-gun unit.

'We set off up the road in an extended artillery column and were immediately strafed by the Italians. We were caught unawares and we'd no training in what to do. When we got to Belchite we met refugees streaming away. The place was dead – completely evacuated and almost destroyed. We were told to go in and hold it. We were in the direct line of the fascist advance and could see about a hundred Italian tanks in the distance on the north side of Belchite. We had some anti-tank backup behind us. We were given no orders to retreat and we'd no cover at all. The tanks kept coming and coming with the fascists behind them.

'The lads in the anti-tank squad were singing "Hold the fort 'till we come." We still had no orders to retreat. Finally we did retreat back into the olive groves, and there was Paddy O'Sullivan I'd known in the IRA, wearing his black beret and calmly directing operations. He was killed later on in the battle. We were still trying to hold on, knowing we were outflanked. The position was indefensible.

'The bullets were hitting the wall behind us, explosive bullets, too. There was just no cover – you lay down and fired as you could. A lot of lads were killed there. When we finally got the order to retreat we were told to hold another position about two kilometres away.

'After we moved out the Moors arrived and they slaughtered everything in sight. All the wounded we hadn't managed to get out, they killed, along with the doctors. They took no prisoners. I remember a friend of mine called Evans had to be abandoned with a bullet in his chest. We heard them shooting the prisoners. The Moors could do what they liked then – they raped, burned, murdered, looted. Later on they had to toe the line, and when I was in San Sebastián prison some of them were there too for doing the very things they had been encouraged to do in action.

'I'm told the Moors were frightened of the International Brigades – quite unjustifiably.

'Our weapons weren't too bad, some were quite good. They were mainly Russian – Mexicansky, as they were called. The position we retreated to from Belchite wasn't much better. The ground was so hard and rocky you could only dig a sixteen-inch trench and you got strafed all the time. You could hear the screaming of the Stukas as they dived. It was nerve-racking, not having any proper cover, but it was impossible to dig in.

'The retreat continued. Sam Wild was in command, and at one time we were trapped between fascist territory and no-man's-land and he decided to split us up and send us back in two patrols, and send us back to the main force two ways, in the hope that some of us would get back. I volunteered to stay, and he told me to get the hell out as I'd got a bad cold . . .'

Joe Norman found the whole situation confusing. 'Small villages were fought for, taken and then lost again by both sides. There was much actual hand-to-hand fighting. Sam Wild, Bobby Walker, Harry Dobson and myself walked into a fascist patrol of about ten armed officers and men just outside Belchite. They wanted all our things – pens, watches and so on – and they were so keen to get them they over-reached themselves.

'It made Bobby Walker really mad and we got away under cover of a punch-up in the darkness. Harry Dobson thumped one bloke with a tin of corned beef.

'On 31 March we went to fight the fascist breakthrough at Gandesa. We'd lost our observer, and so I took three of the men and set off to observe the enemy some 300 yards in front of the battalion. We got the drop on two enemy patrols and sent the information back, then, around the next bend, hell opened up in front of us.

'There were tanks, machine guns, artillery and rifle fire, a full-scale battle on all sides. The attack swept around us

111

before we could blink, leaving us in the rear of the enemy. When I looked down again from where I was hiding, I looked straight down into an Italian gun turret. A voice was shouting something to the effect that we should lay down our arms. We had no option. The olive groves on both sides of the road were swarming with advancing fascists. The night before, the battalion lay in those olive groves when we took over from the Lister Brigade. What we did not know was that the Listers' line had broken and they had pulled out, leaving us to face the full-scale attack of the Nationalists. We heard the tide of battle rolling away from us – it was very lonely.'

'Our gun was so new,' said Bill Feeley, 'that it still had the cap on the nozzle and we didn't have time to take it off in that retreat – we just fired through it. The bloke in charge died, I think, at Gandesa. Anyway, I took charge. Then I saw a tank coming and I wished I'd had some anti-tank training and some proper anti-tank equipment, but we'd nothing. When the tanks came we just kept firing, but we were very exposed and I said, "Look, chaps, we'd better get back a bit, it's a bit dodgy here," so we moved back a bit. Then we got the tank. I set fire to it with machine-gun bullets. It was there on the road – so near I could have reached out and touched it – then it burst into flames. We were still fighting, you see. We didn't know the battalion had gone off, so we'd stayed there firing our gun. That was the day Wally Tapsell got it.

'After we'd destroyed the tank we thought, it's a bit bloody quiet. All the noise had stopped except for our gun. We thought, where's the battalion? Then we realized they'd all gone – there was nobody there. We started back along the road, dragging our machine gun with us, and every now and then we'd stop and fire it. We were real sitting ducks. At one time a group of fascist troops looked as if they were coming to get us, then someone obviously told them to leave us alone and take no bloody notice. Then another tank chased us and we hid in a ditch.

'We could hear its commander shouting up the hill. We

112

still had the gun three quarters of the way up, but in the end we had to leave it. It was quite an adventure, but it's rather muddled as you weren't exactly thinking of how best to write it all down at the time.'

Bob Cooney found even Teruel, 'where at least at one time we'd had a luxury dugout', preferable to the Aragón offensive. 'It was a holocaust at Belchite. We went through a whole series of dreadful battles with a new company which had only just been sent up. The only word to describe it was a holocaust.

'Belchite was really something. The line had broken and the army was in retreat and we had to take up a vantage point to cover it. We lay there firing, on top of a little low house, and behind us we could see the bullets bouncing off the stones. I finally ended up behind a low stone wall, thanks to Sam and three other lads who were covering for me. It got so muddled that it was hard to hit the fascists and not our lads which were in front of them – it was difficult to get the rifle sights right.

'We fought yard by yard and it was very orderly. We finally got out of Belchite down a dry water channel. I remember George Fletcher turning to me and saying, "God, this is pretty hot" – he'd been wounded for the fourth time. We were in an absolutely hopeless position. It was absolutely flat country. Those in command didn't know the ground, and I believe we were sent to defend Belchite on a map reference only.

'We were under continual heavy bombardment and we kept getting encircled. I remember we got to the last of the cognac ration. There was a good crowd of us leaving Belchite, moving away from being encircled, we seemed to escape from one lousy position only to end up in another. We did one trek of fifty-seven kilometres without water or a rest, carrying heavy packs and hampered by strings and strings of refugees also escaping. The whole thing culminated at Calaceite, with the defence of Gandesa.

'The front line had actually broken on 31 March. It's been said that Calaceite was so disastrous because we didn't take the elementary precaution of putting scouts out. We did, we sent them out before we did anything, but we were just *racing* to get there. All around us were the signs of people having retreated in haste, and as we got round one corner we walked into some tanks. George Fletcher told us to take to the high ground and get by as best we could. There were hordes of yelling Italians and some of our lads got held down.

'Jack Coward, who was there, said to me, "Let's get the hell out of this lot." It was every man for himself, and we got out as best we could. I remember seeing some Yugoslav soldier just standing around without moving. I asked him why, and he said if we move we'll be killed, and I told him that if we didn't bloody move we'll all be killed. So we moved – the Yugoslavs too. We crawled up and down the hillside terraces, hoping we'd reach the top of the hill and get to the wooded side and into cover.

'Suddenly we ran slap into a fascist patrol and they said, "Hands up!" As they said this another patrol arrived with a whole lot of our lads they'd just captured, and in the excitement that followed, I managed to get away. I could see our lads being frisked before they were marched away.

'We managed to reach the wood, a few of us, but a hell of a lot of lads were captured there, a hell of a lot – a quarter of the battalion. It's been said since, too, that we didn't conduct the retreat according to the rules of war. If we had, they'd have been straight across the bloody Ebro. They didn't get across only because we conducted ourselves in this stupid, amateurish fashion.

'We kept on going, and as it was a very fluid, mobile front, we picked up every abandoned weapon we came across. The area must have been full of little groups of Britons fighting as best they could – the battalion had got completely split up.

'Anyway, eventually we did meet up with some of the other lads. We were bloody hungry. We'd had nothing to eat since 31 March, and then it was a piece of meat that looked as if it had been shaved off. We reached the Mora de

114

Ebro, having had two meals in three days, and were told to hold a position in the line again and hold up the fascist advance for a day to give time for the Republican lines to reform.

'We held this hill with what arms we'd got, trying not to waste ammunition. There was a hell of a lot of fire there. But we yelled as we fired and made so much noise we convinced the fascists that there were a hell of a lot of us there and they actually held off. We were then told to wait until dark, and then take a small party and go down the road to the river. It was a hell of a long way and we were exhausted. So I said, "Remember the hunger marches, lads. If our feet won't get us there our voices will, and whatever happens we'll bloody *sing* as if we were one hell of a column marching along." Suddenly as we marched we saw these bloody lights coming towards us. Do you know who it was? Sam Wild on a lorry. He'd got away – what a reunion. He'd been hurt again, too. That man was wounded five times in Spain.

'So with Sam at our head we headed for the Ebro. We'd a wonderful scout with us and he got us there very cleverly. It was a long way and we slept uneasily all one night as we just couldn't carry on any further. Then we went down this very, very steep hill to the Ebro. We knew we had to cross it and didn't know how, but luckily it wasn't too deep and we waded across, but it was very, very cold. We were warmly greeted when we arrived – they'd given us up for gonners.

'I was made battalion commissar then as George Fletcher had died.'

Bob was one of the fortunate ones who escaped. The majority of the Scots lads from Glasgow, who had survived Brunete and Teruel, walked into trouble in the Aragón offensive.

George Murray remembers that 'Ben Glazer and I were the absolute rearguard going out of Gandesa. It wasn't bravery on our part, though Ben was a very brave man, as he was a bundle of nerves. He says calmly, though, "We'll have to get out of here," and I said, "Fine, Ben, and just where are we going to go?" We'd been twenty-four hours without food and hadn't noticed it until things quietened down. There were a lot of Italian tanks about.

'We looked around. There was nobody there. They'd all retreated, so there we were, just the two of us, just like that. I woke up that day with the sun shining and I thought, where's everybody? and that's where they were – they'd gone. So we set off to find them. I said we'd need to do a wee bit of orienteering without maps, but we had to go somewhere.'

William Josephs, retreating too, remembers passing a motor bike 'by the side of the road by the side of which was a plate with two fried eggs on it. Then over the brow of a hill came a tank and my mate said, "That's a Nazi tank," and I said he couldn't know that and carried on. Across the road I saw a lovely army blanket, and I said to him, "I'll have that," so I lifted it up and the next thing I knew a fascist soldier rushes up to me, and I don't know who was more afraid, me or him, and he says, "*Maños arriba!*" I said, "Don't shout at me, I don't know the language," and I said "*Escossas*" or something I thought sounded like Scottish in Spanish. He still came at me so I settled for "*Inglesa*" and I realized I'd put my hands up.'

'The war ended for us there,' says Garry McCartney. 'We retreated fast but not fast enough. It was a most vicious action, that last stand at Gandesa. I have the strongest recollections of a comrade on one machine gun at one side of the church where we were fighting, and Barney Shields on the other side of the church. It was a fairly commanding height where this church was and Sam Wild had received orders finally that we should retire. We never retreated, incidentally, we always retired . . .

'We were giving the comrades fire to the best of our ability and we could see them going down this lane, and as they did we saw the dust spurting up from the fire of the fascists. They were very, very close, and I shouted to Barney that we must try and get the guns back. The team I was with – three or four of us – took the gun apart and went down this small lane to join the others, carrying the pieces. The last thing I remember of Barney was hearing him shouting and swearing, and he must have died there as he didn't come. He refused to, he just stayed at his gun, and I never saw him again. We were told recently he'd been buried in a military cemetery at Alicante, but I don't see how – it was miles away.

'It was just a whole mass of retreating actions, the Aragón, fighting during the day and retreating at night, trying to get back, under instructions, to the north-east. We were a very tired, very dishevelled group of men. We were so exhausted that when the enemy planes came over and we were told to take cover, many of us just fell asleep as soon as we lay on the ground because we were so overcome with lack of sleep that the noise of bombs and planes just didn't disturb us. This was the experience of all of us on that retreat.

'On the morning we were captured – about 140 of us outside Calaceite – I was with a machine-gun section bringing up the rear. We'd held a high position for about three quarters of an hour, giving covering fire, then we moved back to try and defend what was obviously an even worse position. As we did we walked slap into an ambush of about forty or fifty men of the Italian crack Black Arrow division.'

14   Prisoner

The war did not end, in fact, for those unlucky enough to be captured on the retreat from Gandesa. They were about to experience one of the most harrowing offshoots of the war: imprisonment, with interrogation by the Gestapo.

As Bob Doyle says, one of the reasons they were picked up was their state of exhaustion. 'I've picked crusts off the road and eaten them. Then the lack of sleep got so bad we'd hold on to the back of peasants' carts and sleep as we walked. We lay down to fire in the trenches and slept. Funnily enough, there wasn't much disease, but the lice were a pest.

'On 31 March we'd sent out a dawn patrol which didn't come back, and we were going into a position around a bend of the road but it wasn't a good one. Suddenly there was a dreadful noise getting louder and louder all the time, coming from the valley. Then we were surrounded by thousands of Italian troops, many on motor-cycles with machine guns on their handlebars.

'They told us to put up our hands, but even when we did so they fired through us. There was no alternative but to give up. We were only about twenty feet, too, from some tanks.

'We were then marched with our hands up for about a mile, and as we were going along we saw massive contingents of Italians, including the Black Arrow regiment. As we passed through their ranks they spat on us, poured petrol over us and hit us. Some people were singled out and beaten to get information, including Frank Ryan. We were then

118

told that all communists and socialists and Jews had to step forward. I didn't like the Italians, but having heard of the horrors of the Spanish Civil Guards when I was sailing to and from Spain, I thought it was better we had them.

'At one point they lined us up and stood in front of us with rifles levelled. We all tried to push into the front line so that if we were shot it would be the end, we wouldn't die by degrees. But then they stopped and again asked Frank Ryan to stand out. They beat him when he wouldn't give any information.

'We were then taken to a disused church and crammed in for two days without food, hardly any water, and we had to use the back of the altar as a toilet. From there we were transported to Saragossa where we saw people from the Lister Division being made to stand by the Franco flag. We also saw prisoners in open-air compounds without any shelter at all.

'The first thing we were told was that we had to give the fascist salute or we'd be shot. We argued a lot about it and then compromised on a British salute, although Frank Ryan wouldn't even do that.'

Joe Norman said, 'We were marched off down that road which had been so bitterly fought over, our hands above our heads, tired, hungry and miserable. We did not feel better after we'd been sneered at by a reporter from the *Daily Express*. "You'll all be shot," he told us, encouragingly. We were sitting on the ground in the town square at Gandesa when he came and he started asking questions to which he did not want to hear the answers. Then we were loaded into camions and taken to Saragossa and, after a while, to a concentration camp at San Pedro.

'What a horrible place! It was controlled by the German Gestapo, and more than 600 IBers from twenty different countries were all crammed into one long room. It looked like a dungeon and had walls six foot thick and floors made of stone. Even in the middle of the day the light was so bad you could hardly see to the end of it. We had one thin palliasse between two and no blankets. If anyone had hung on

119

to a blanket, he shared it.

'I decided to form an education committee to take people's minds off things, and classes started in all kinds of subjects – chess, economics, maths, etc. Meanwhile dysentery ran through us all and men died like flies of that and of typhoid and influenza. The sick were taken to an upper floor and thrown on the floor and lay there without help or medicine until they either died or recovered.

'Sometimes if people were seriously ill – and Jesus, were we hungry! – the prison doctor would grovel to the commander for more food. Usually, in the twenty-four hours, you received one eight-ounce loaf, a bowl of hot water with a red pepper floating on the top, and a piece of fish with a few beans. The toilets were shocking. A sunken room, it was, without water or paper. Men started tearing their clothing to use as paper.

'The inevitable happened. The sunken room flooded five feet deep, and in the interests of health volunteers were asked to go and free the blockage. I volunteered with two others, a Canadian and a Scot. I had to dive under all that piss and shit, naked, but we succeeded in clearing the drain and got an extra eight-ounce loaf as a reward. But my two comrades died of typhoid within a week. Five Olympic gold medals wouldn't have been good enough to swap for that loaf of bread. It tasted beautiful – I can still recall the taste of that bread after forty years.

'It was so cold. Such a cold place you can't imagine. I went down with pneumonia and lay shivering and nearly lifeless on the floor of that upper room. I was lucky – they gave me two aspirins. Suddenly it struck me, if I didn't move I'd die, so I got up and staggered away.

'Then the Gestapo got busy. They began to ferret out the officers, and those who had been leading lights in anti-fascist movements were taken away regularly. They were never seen again. Rumours began to circulate that the Republicans had broken through at Saragossa and were advancing on Burgos, and this provoked an uproar in the brigade. The camp committee was besieged with requests for a breakout, but we were sure the rumour had come from the Gestapo to see what we would do. If we broke out we'd all die.

'We were proved right in the end. The Gestapo sent for us one by one to interrogate us about the so-called breakout. I was interrogated by two Gestapo officers, and carried away with bravado I gave them the closed-fist salute. I thought they were going to shoot me on the spot, but after some dirty looks they instructed two Spanish guards to beat me, which they did for some time. At one point I wondered who was making all the noise, and then I realized it was me.

'We had to cope with all kinds of problems. Every Sunday we had to attend church parade and prisoners were forced there by fixed bayonets. At the end of the service we were supposed to give the fascist salute. We all wanted to refuse, but we were told to do it rather than die for the sake of it as it would be quite meaningless. So we all did, except for our German comrades who refused. They just stood there and refused. Armed guards swarmed all over them, bashing their heads with rifle butts until they were unconscious and bleeding. Then they were carried away and were never seen again.

'Then one morning, between two and three o'clock, the guards roused up most of the camp committee, including me. They said nothing to us. They lined us up against a wall and also lined up a firing squad. They kept us there for about an hour, pressed against that wall, then they took us back in. The following day they repeated the treatment. We never discovered why. Most of us were shattered with shock and cold. It was quite a while before we could take it in that we would be eating our red-pepper soup again.'

Bob Doyle, too, was ill treated. 'We were continually beaten. We were beaten with sticks and rifle butts, we were beaten if we broke ranks and to make us break ranks; before we woke in the morning; when we went to get our food.

'The Gestapo interrogated all the prisoners and also measured us all, especially our heads, and gave us tests. They were trying to prove we were abnormal.

'Our clothing was taken away and I spent a long time just wrapped in a blanket. The Gestapo asked all kinds of crazy questions like how old were you when you had your first woman, was she a prostitute, as well as why did you come to Spain? The Gestapo didn't actually beat us themselves, they got the Spaniards to do it, but the Germans were tortured and beaten, and then had to sign forms to say they wanted to go back. This was to prove to non-interventionists that they were going of their own free will.

'They got back, were terribly tortured and disappeared. The Czechs had a bad time, too, especially those from the Sudetenland. Germany had invaded by then and they were told that and treated accordingly.

'Our treatment was brutal, demoralizing and disgusting, and it was a deliberate strategy to break us down and prove we were subhuman to have fought in the IB. Some did break, some just gave up and pined away and died. Anyone seriously ill was just left to die among the others with no treatment. At the end they'd disappear and the next you knew you'd be told they'd died and they'd make a coffin out of fishcrates and you'd line up to see them buried. Whatever religion or none, you were told they'd died asking for the last rites of the Catholic Church.

'In that prison in San Sebastián we saw a wall in the exercise yard which was nearly cut in two with bullet holes from rifles and machine guns. We were told that over 4,000 prisoners had been shot there. They were still shooting prisoners then. I used to converse through a hole with a Basque prisoner in a cell above me and he told me. He knew he was going to be shot. I heard a scuffle one morning and he died shouting, '*Viva la República!*' Those prisoners in some cells had little windows and could see others allowed to play football – they were awaiting execution, too.

'In Ireland, the priesthood supported Franco. But there were two priests in there, survivors of a batch of twenty-six from Guernica who had refused to say from the pulpit that the Republicans, and not Franco, had burned Guernica.'

Before Garry McCartney reached the same prison, 'the

soldiers that picked us three up took us just behind the lines. They seemed to be discussing something with their officers and it sounded like they wanted to shoot us. I didn't feel all that worried at the time, I was just sad that this was to be the end of it all. But they didn't, of course. Then a frightfully respectable Italian officer came up and said, "I say, you chaps, you're English, I must have a wee chat with you," terribly well-spoken. All around us were guns, thousands and thousands of guns. We'd had nothing. Then we were taken to their commanding officers up in the hills.'

He and George Drever, also from Glasgow, 'travelled to the final prison on a train, in cattle trucks. Before we got on the train we were given a tin of sardines, and that was all we had for three days. There were all kinds of nationalities on that train. At every station women came to give us water, and I remember there was one huge Polish man who was always able to get to this water. He had it at every stop. Lying on the floor were men too sick to get up, and I said to him, "Look, if you don't pass over some of that water I'll kick you in the balls, and I'll keep on kicking you until you do." It must have had some effect because after that he handed over some water.'

From time to time the men in prison were cleaned up and paraded in front of visitors and foreign press to give the appearance that they were being well treated. 'I remember getting a visit from Princess Victoria and her attendants,' said William Josephs. 'As she passed she made a remark about "the scum of Britain" and I said, "Aye, I can see them following on behind you." '

The Gestapo questioned McCartney and Josephs too, 'and one day they arrived with cameras and took pictures, especially of those lads who were obviously Jewish, and of the Negroes, too. When Jimmy Goldsmith next to me was singled out, I stepped out too," remembers Garry McCartney, 'and they took my picture. That night we were all sitting down to have our "meal", and there was an orange, and they came round to all those who'd had their pictures taken and took the oranges away!'

The filth was disgusting. 'A few old dry closets to cope with 700 men. You can imagine it. Lice were a problem, as they had been throughout the war. You'd walk about before the dawn, because it was freezing, then you'd take off your trousers and jacket when the sun came up and start delousing them. You'd kill as many lice as you could and put the clothes back on again. By night-time, of course, they were back there biting.'

George Drever remembers the hunger. 'Every morning you'd be given a loaf of bread and it was supposed to last the day, but often you'd eat it as you were so hungry. I remember then this lad who had to go to the hospital – which was just another shed – and he was there two days. Each day they left his bread and we ate his bread too.

'One night these guards came in and grabbed me to help carry a Spanish lad on a stretcher to hospital. Four of us carried him to the hospital and it was a struggle as we were pretty weak by this time. We got him to the hospital, and it was strange to go in the streets and see people walking about free out there. Anyway, we got to the hospital and the doctor said, "Poor boy, there's nothing we can do for him."

'The most important thing was that there was a blanket over him, a kind of travelling-rug thing. It was absolutely filthy. It had vomit on it and all kinds of things, but I wanted to get this blanket so I whipped it and took it back. It's the sort of blanket that if you saw it now it would make you heave just to look at it.

'As to lice, there was a Welsh comrade in San Pedro who had lost an arm which made it impossible for him to effectively delouse himself. So we used to have to delouse him. Now it's bad enough killing one's *own* lice, but to kill some-one else's lice . . . at least, I suppose they might have been one's own lice, but you didn't know.'

Only one Briton is known to have been shot, however. His name was Jimmy Rutherford and he had been repatriated from Spain in May 1937 and then returned to fight again. Under a League of Nations edict any Brigader who was captured, repatriated and then caught again would be shot. All the Scots lads and Bob Doyle and Joe Norman have stories of what happened to Jimmy when he turned up in the prison camp.

'Jimmy,' according to Joe Norman, 'had been captured in the early days of the war, had been sentenced to death and then escaped. When he got to the prison he gave an assumed name. When the Gestapo lined them up for fingerprints when they got there, Jimmy was in trouble. So we had a quick discussion and I was pushed into the fingerprint line. We hoped he could get away with it and held our breath for two days, but it was no good. He must have known he was finished, but he never showed it. He was a brave boy.'

According to Garry McCartney and Bob Doyle, Rutherford was recognized when a visiting delegation came around. 'We'd been washed and given a meal,' says Doyle. 'As it turned out they wanted to impress some pro-Franco journalists. I think some came from the *Daily Telegraph* and *New York Times*. We were paraded in front of them. Then suddenly one of the Spanish nationalists with them, Merry del Val, saw Jimmy, who was calling himself Smalls, and said, "Don't I know you?" Jimmy said no, as he knew he'd be shot if he was recognized. But they picked him out and later on he was.'

'When del Val came, Jimmy Rutherford was standing close to me at the time,' says Garry. 'He passed Jimmy and said, immediately, "Have you been in Spain before?" Jimmy was under another name, of course, and he said no, it was his first time in Spain. This was obviously not believed and some eight or nine weeks later he was taken from us. We heard from the representatives of the British government, who visited us three or four times in San Pedro, that he had been shot under an edict of the League of Nations which said that anybody who had been repatriated as a prisoner would not take part in any further action.'

One man who had a remarkable prison story is no longer alive to tell it: Jack Coward. In Bob Doyle's words: 'He was captured in Spain at Gandesa, but then escaped and found himself behind the fascist lines. He fought with the Spanish guerrillas, but got captured again. He was terrified they'd discover his identity as they had his identification and prints and so on and, already captured once, he'd have been shot.

'So he feigned deaf and dumbness. He managed to keep it up, God knows how, and pass himself off as Spanish. Everyone thought he was dead. When he got back he was in a dreadful state. He had not spoken for months and months, dare hardly sleep in case he spoke in his sleep, pretending to be illiterate and shellshocked. He got away in the end, and to the port of Vigo, and a British ship smuggled him aboard.

'The first time I saw him he looked very pitiable indeed. He'd gone white-haired and he was ill. But he got better, of course, and later he led the famous seamens' strike.

'Actually, while I was in prison, I was also reported dead. It was the second time. I'd been reported dead in the Baltic in the First War and have my name still on my local war memorial at home.'

George Drever summed up the feeling of most of the men who were taken prisoner: 'The only thing that grieves me over my time in Spain was that I was taken prisoner. The more so under the conditions in which we had to live – it was a very dramatic experience.

'We went there to try and do something for Spain. Lads were wounded and lads were killed, and some of us became prisoners-of-war. The feeling I have about it is something I've never been able to get out of my system – the feeling of frustration and inadequacy. The question was brought up at the fortieth anniversary of the war, about Jimmy Rutherford, that the Communist Party should never have let him go back again. But I said that if I had been taken prisoner earlier in the war and released, I would certainly have gone straight back.

'It wouldn't have been a question of the party saying you should or should not go back, it would have been a matter for the individual. I would just have to have gone back.'

15   Behind the Lines

While those who were taken prisoner were coping as well as they could with the hardships they had to endure, the shattered remnants of the British Battalion were preparing themselves for what was to be their last battle: the crossing of the Ebro in the summer of 1938.

But there were two other small bodies of British volunteers in Spain. There were the men who went and worked as ambulance drivers and stretcher bearers, and the women who nursed or worked on the administrative side, rustling up food supplies, clothing, medical equipment and so on.

George and Nan Green both went to Spain. Nan, who is now secretary of the International Brigade Association, came back alone. Her husband was killed on the last day on which the British were involved in fighting in Spain. He had survived the whole war as an ambulance driver, only becoming a fighting soldier at the very end of it.

He left behind, in letters, one of the few accounts of what it was like to be working with the wounded brought in from the field and the conditions under which those who were involved had to work:

Our own hospital is a little lower down the hill, a more modern monastery building with horrid stucco decoration. As a hospital it's not bad except that the water supply is a bit inadequate until we get our own emergency dynamo working and the stairs are steep and bad for stretcher carrying.

These are mainly carried by local boys whom we co-opt

with no time to train them properly. To make just four journeys, each time with a bed to the top floor, leaves me as distressed as if I'd run a mile and I'm a good deal thinner and fitter than when I left England.

We work dourly, saying hardly a word, cleaning out rooms, scrubbing, wiring, fixing lights in the theatres and in the area downstairs which is used for reception. Again that is a bad word, since it 'makes you think rather of a social function than a room where the first clean-up takes place, bloody trousers are ripped off quivering thighs and the wounded are sorted into severe, not so severe – and dead.

We are stealing labour from other departments while labour is stolen from our own, while being appealed to to find this or that in the darkness – such as a load of stuff which was definitely loaded on a certain truck and can't be found or, more incredibly, some personal luggage which some unbelievable person has found time to think about or has mislaid. We stare in amazement and reach for our gun.

We do not notice the coming of darkness except to be annoyed at the inconvenience of the failing light and nobody notices the dawn. We drink hot coffee and wonder how the cook will continue to feed properly more than 300 people from that small kitchen and presently, after a lot more work and the ambulances have all left for the front – and me with no vehicle still – I find myself doing all sorts of odd jobs, putting tents up and looking for people that other people can't find.

Then I found myself appointed as a theatre orderly to Tudor Hart's theatre. This may not sound onerous but includes the duties of anaesthetist, all-in wrestler, stage manager, settler of disputes between sister and surgeon, selector of raw material from reception and secretary. Also, occasionally, assistant surgeon in a consultative capacity when everyone else is too tired to use common sense.

We worked for two days and nights with never more

than two hours' sleep and you can't imagine the tiredness of it and yet the feeling of being buoyed up by the knowledge that the hospital is full of wounded men who depend on us and who may already have waited for six or twelve hours before getting to hospital.

Some of them die on the operating table. One man had an awful smashed leg. A piece of shell had cut through, splintering the bone and nerve endings and we worked like hell to save it and patch up the holes. Twice, before he went under as I was giving him the anaesthetic, he asked whether he must lose his leg and I said no, he'd be walking about on it in a couple of months' time. So we mended it and cleaned it and took pieces of metal out and we put on a beautiful plaster cast. Hart does some lovely plaster work. We spent altogether about four hours on it and took him down in triumph to the ward.

And next day – he'd been out on the hillside for twelve hours before they brought him in – he'd got gas gangrene and we had to carry him up again. The plaster was crawling with maggots and the wound stank as only gangrene can stink and he was dead as mutton from the hip down on his left side. On the table he was patient and kind to us as only Spaniards can be, and just before he went under he asked the same question again and I couldn't answer him and didn't need to because he already knew.

He closed his eyes and we fought to get the leg off before the rot got any higher – and you can see the stuff spreading under your eyes – and after I'd taken the stinking limb down to the fire and got back to the theatre, he came to before we got him off the table, although I'd been trying to get rid of him before his eyes could see what we'd done to him.

He thanked us and said 'Salud!' as his stretcher went out of the door. But he cried a little afterwards in the ward they said 'because one gets fond of one's legs'. And that man lives.

But another man came in the same day with both feet smashed up and the same unmistakable stink. We took his feet off and burned them and plastered what was left and sent him down. Twelve hours later it was obvious we hadn't taken enough off and he came up again and moaned at us. He took ether and his pulse was awful as he was badly shocked from the day before. So we gave him a blood transfusion and he improved and we took his leg off at the hip and gave him another injection and then his body revolted at this awful cutting, cutting and he just died.

That's about all I've done in the last 150 hours – cleaning wounds ready for operation, holding the heads of men who were suffering with incredible patience, shaving hairy Spanish legs and testicles, falling down on a mattress for two hours of oblivion, going down for coffee and meeting Mrs Murphy who's the nurse in charge of the ward to which our cases go. She is all in.

She has a son at Bedales and during the last few hours she has seen too many mothers' sons carried with sheets over staring eyes down to the wash house at the bottom of the garden. We speak bitterly of gangrene as a personal enemy.

When Nan Green was asked to go, her husband having gone on ahead, 'I had a great conflict because I already had two children. I sat up for a whole night thinking about whether I should go or not. I was largely able to go due to the children's grandfather who I knew would love them and look after them.

'When he heard that George had gone – and we'd told nobody that he was going – he said in his Lancashire voice, "If I was twenty years younger I'd go myself."

'I was also fortunate in that a friend who had been wounded in Spain offered to support them at school. I didn't intend to stay very long, but I stayed longer than I had intended because there was so much to do. I stayed thirteen months and didn't come back until the International Brigades came back.

'I was in a hospital in the beginning. I became secretary to a large hospital which was based in a monastery which had been abandoned by the monks, and then I moved to be the administrator of a large hospital for convalescents. It was right up in the mountains and had hot springs so they could have hot baths at any time as it was bubbling out of the ground.

'I was there for several months, and then I went to a hospital where I didn't think I was any use because the staff there were hostile to foreigners, and later the doctors turned out to be sympathetic to the fascists and I heard later that when the Nationalist troops marched in they got their blue shirts out from under the bed and gave the fascist salute.

'They were incompetent and tried to stop me doing my job, which was looking after a small group of English nurses who had come out later. So I left there just at the time of the fascist breakthrough – when they cut Spain in two and got right through to the coast – and managed to reach the north and became secretary to the Divisional Medical Officer of the 35th Division, and I went right through the Ebro campaign until the September.

'I had a rubber stamp tied round my neck, without which he couldn't sign anything, and I had a big bag of tea and a small primus stove so that I could make tea, day and night, for everybody when I wasn't doing my statistical work. I came out two or three weeks after the brigades had been withdrawn, having stayed on because they couldn't find anyone to replace the small number of foreigners who were doing our kind of jobs.

'I think probably the most important thing I did was to serve tea, but I did do a lot of statistical work on wounds, what caused them, what people died of and so on. We had some kind of a headquarters in which I slept in a cleaned-out pigsty, and near by were four front-line medical posts. Every day, at four o'clock, they'd draw a line under that day's injured and send the records up to me, and I would extract the type of wounds, whether the patient survived, and if he did how long it took him to recover and go back to the front so that we could trace their progress.

'We could also deduce other things. If you had a whole lot of head injuries from mortar fire, you knew more steel helmets were needed. In the 1939–45 war, Dr Douglas Jolly, who had been at that front, came and asked me to dig out of my memory what I could about all this as he would find it useful in Italy.

'I saw my husband only a few times while I was in Spain. He was in the first hospital I was in as he'd been injured. He'd been driving his ambulance and it had developed a fault and he'd got under it to see what was wrong when some petrol ran down his arm inside his sleeeve and it froze and injured his skin badly. It was purely by chance that we both turned up there.

'Then I met him after we crossed the Ebro – I like to think I was the first woman across the Ebro, but I'm not quite sure as other people have claimed it – the night after the crossing when he arrived with some of the people from the battalion who had got away.

'Then I saw him again just before he died. He'd been wounded in the head and he was really ready to go back to the front, but like all of us he had skin disease – you only had to scratch it and it would suppurate – but he had it very badly, and he was in hospital where they were trying to cure him. But when he heard that the brigades were going to be sent home, he demanded to be released from hospital so that he could finish the battle with them.

'He wanted to finish the war with them. He was absolutely convinced that the armaments the Russians had sent and which were the other side of the French frontier would be sent across in time, that the French couldn't possibly see fascism win. So he came through the medical headquarters four or five days before his death, and we thought we would only meet again in England. So I like to think he died full of confidence. I think it was a good way to die. He believed it must come right. He was doing what he knew he had to do and he believed the Republic would be victorious.

'So I've not felt sorry for him as a young man, dying at the age of thirty-four, doing what he wanted to do and feeling

132

they were bound to win. So there's a young man forever confident. But he was killed in the very last hour of the last day. On 22 September they were supposed to be withdrawn, but later on the 22nd and into the 23rd they were asked to go back into the lines. I've never discovered exactly where – but a year or two later someone sent me a little diagram of the lines and how they were in diagonal slit trenches at the time. George was in charge of a machine gun when the Italians came over and threw in hand grenades. They got out, but when they had done so George wasn't there, so I think that's how he died. I like to think he died quickly. But for the next six months I didn't know if he were alive or dead. It was a terrible time. It was the May or June of 1939 that I finally got a certificate to say he'd died. It was a time I'd not want anybody to go through.

'I think we were right to go. If Spain had been helped to weather those next few months, the Second War may never have happened.

'In a practical way, some good came out of what happened in Spain. I was given a silly book recently about a vet who used a plaster treatment which was invented during the war in Spain. Now that treatment was invented out of necessity. We were always desperately short of any kind of medical supplies at all. A wound which was suppurating or messy just used to have plaster slapped on it. Then a few days later, when they took it off, all the infection and things disappeared with it. Even though the plaster became appalling, it absorbed the infection from the wound, which eventually became clean. It was used a lot in the Second War.

'The other thing was the blood transfusion, and surgery right at the front. Instead of rushing people back, because the terrain was so awful, we had the first operating theatres right at the front so that the injured didn't have the agony of being driven over appalling roads and die of shock.

'It was early in the Spanish War that they began to use blood banks. But when we crossed the Ebro on the pontoon bridges – because the proper bridges had been bombed down – there were sometimes days when the blood couldn't get up to the front. So anybody who was more or less sedentary like me used to be sent for to give blood and I gave a great deal of blood in quite a short time.

'I'm lucky in that I have one of those groups which they didn't have to bother about who to give it to. After you'd given blood you were given a little bit of paper entitling you to a tin of condensed milk and an egg, but we never got them, of course, they just weren't there. But I remember one occasion, I think it was the second time in a fortnight I'd been sent for, which was very moving. Those who have only given blood in a hospital and don't see where it goes don't know how lovely it is to lie down beside the man who needs it, whose face has gone ghastly white and there's no colour in his lips, and you lie there and your blood goes into him and you see the colour go back into his face. It's simply marvellous. If everybody could do that once there'd be many more volunteers.

'I thought in those early days of the Ebro offensive that we would turn the tide and drive them back, and we would have done if only we'd had the armaments. You always knew whose planes were in the sky. If you saw a plane and the air was full of the puffs of smoke from anti-aircraft guns, that was one of ours. If there were only a few puffs, then it was theirs as we had virtually no anti-aircraft artillery. If only we'd had those arms from the other side of the border in France. . .

'But I'll never regret it. As for George – well, he died like a bird who dies in flight – it just keeps on flying.'

16   Across the Ebro – and Home

'Evil lifts a hand and the heads of the flowers fall –
The pall of the hero who by the Ebro bleeding
Feeds with his blood the stones that rise and call,
Tall as any man, "No Pasarán!"'
                        – George Barker, 'Elegy for Spain'

Following the collapse of the Aragón front and the division of Republican Spain, the Republican leadership begged France to reopen the frontier. They also begged once again for arms, but the non-intervention policy was strictly adhered to although the Germans and Italians were pouring equipment into Nationalist Spain. By July 1938, the Nationalists held three quarters of the country. The Republicans launched a final, diversionary attack, to try and save the city of Valencia. It was decided to force a crossing of the Ebro about seventy miles from the sea. Had they had sufficient men and equipment, the course of the war may have been changed even at this late stage for, against all expectations, the attack was extremely successful. It caught Franco unawares and damaged the morale of the Nationalists at a time when they considered the war as good as won. But success was impossible for the Republic without sufficient men, arms, basic equipment or transport. The tide was to roll against them for the last time. Meanwhile, during the Ebro battle, the Munich Conference was taking place, and it was during this and while the League of Nations was meeting for what would be the last time, that

Juan Negrín proposed the withdrawal of the International Brigades in a vain hope that Germany and Italy would do likewise.

*

Very few of the Britons who fought in Spain survived to cross the Ebro. Those who did had struggled back to the Republican lines through a tide of the Nationalist advance and the rout of the Republic in the Aragón. Sometimes they turned up on their own after days of wandering, sometimes they clung together in small groups. It was left to Sam Wild and Bob Cooney to rebuild what remained of the British Battalion with those who managed to return and the wounded discharged from hospital.

On 24 July 1938, Juan Negrín told the Republican War Council in Barcelona that Valencia would fall unless there was a diversionary attack elsewhere. The decision was made to recross the Ebro, which would not only divert Franco but could possibly restore communications between Catalonia and what remained of Republican Spain. A new Army of the Ebro was constituted under the command of Colonel José Modesto.

At a quarter past midnight on 24–5 July, with no moon, Modesto took his army across the hundred-yard-wide river. The first stages of the attack were extremely successful, and Lister, with his Vth Army Corps, advanced twenty-five miles to reach once again the town of Gandesa.

The main fighting took place there. The town was assaulted day and night during the rest of the month, and on 1 August the XVth Brigade launched a fierce attack on Hill 481. The casualties were again high as they had been the last time the tide of battle rolled round Gandesa in March. The brigade, and the British Battalion with it, failed to take either Hill 481 or Gandesa, but in spite of this the Republican advance continued until the end of the first week in August.

Once Franco had recovered from his surprise, he retaliated in strength. He first launched a massive aerial bombardment, concentrating almost his entire air force on the Ebro. The Republican engineers performed amazing feats of skill and endurance as they continually repaired the pontoon bridges their army had thrown across the river. It is estimated that Nationalist aircraft dropped some 10,000 pounds of bombs on the bridges every day.

By mid-August, the Republican advance was finished. They were dogged by lack of arms and even vehicles. Weary soldiers had to march to the front on foot as there were hardly any lorries.

As at Teruel, the accounts of those who saw the Ebro fighting are sketchy because of the way the British Battalion was deployed. It saw the initial crossing of the river and the fighting which followed, but on 6 August, after thirteen days of continuous action, the British were put into reserve as the Republican army found itself being relentlessly pushed back over ground for which it had bitterly fought. After eight days in reserve, the British Battalion returned to the line and again fought in a fierce battle for a hill, this time Hill 666 in the Sierra de Pandols, during which they took heavy casualties. Sam Wild, commanding the British in the action, was wounded again but refused to leave. On 26 August the British were pulled out once more and placed in reserve. On 22 September orders were received that they, and the XVth Brigade, were to go once again to the front. At the same time news reached them that all the brigades were to be pulled out of Spain. After hearing the news, the British Battalion decided to fight one last time. It was a decision which was to cost them heavily.

'We did a lot of training before we crossed the Ebro,' remembers Bob Cooney. 'What I remember most is the feeling of great optimism and hope that everybody had. We were highly confident.

'One of the most moving things that ever happened to me happened when we crossed the Ebro. An old, old man saw the troops coming and he came to have a closer look. As we

137

came along the road, carrying the banner of the British Battalion, he knelt down in the road, took up the hem of the flag and kissed it.

'It's fortunate we didn't know what was in store. It would have been a cheek to think we could succeed if we'd seen what they'd got waiting for us. I remember thinking, Jesus Christ, I'm going to get back and then I'll take a nice young wife, I'll get married.

'We went into action on August Bank Holiday Monday – what a day – and seven times my lads advanced up that hill and were driven back. Sam had a field telephone, and he was talking to a general in charge of the operations and telling him that the fascists were only twenty-five yards away. He was told, "You'll be wiped out if you stay, you can't retreat, the only thing you can do is to get to the top of the hill." I heard Sam shout, "For Christ's sake, this isn't a film, it's a bloody battle!" After this battle – the battle of Hill 481 – Modesto called the British Battalion the shock battalion of the whole army. Tony Maguire, one of our boxing champions, got to the top of the parapet of a Spanish trench, and they called out in Spanish, "Surrender!" "Surrender be fucked," he replied and emptied his automatic into them.

'We were in reserve at Hill 481, plugging a hole in the line. We were then pushed back and back, and it was on the evening of 22 September that a call came through on the field telephone saying that Negrín had just announced that the International Brigades were to be withdrawn. But, we were told, we should go back into the line that night. I was told not to tell the lads that they were going to be withdrawn altogether, just that they would be withdrawn for a prolonged rest.

'We thought if we'd told them, they might have gone into battle in a terrible spirit. Added to which, they had just been the victim of a dreadful mistake when two of our own planes came over and strafed us instead of the Nationalists. We went into battle the next day into a barrage of artillery and we were completely outnumbered.

'We had to retreat down a steep slope, trying to carry

quite a lot of wounded. Shells were bursting around us, they were giving us hell, when I remember one lad, who'd been a wine merchant, turning to me in the midst of all this and saying, "I don't think I could ever be a communist, communists believe in violence." It seemed a strange thing to say at that particular moment. He then got a wound in the back and said, "Comrades, don't leave me." We managed to get him back all right.'

Sam Wild, who had seen so much continuous action and been five times wounded, and who commanded the battalion in its final months, says that, 'Right until the end I never thought the fascists would win. I never thought they would. It sounds crazy.

'We had learned a good deal. We learned, for example, that it was more important to locate and destroy the enemy's water supply than to anticipate what would happen if enemy tanks crossed a certain part of the terrain.

'What tends to be forgotten, too, by the strategists and experts and those who make a study of warfare is that the most important thing is the morale and ideals and beliefs of the ordinary people, the ordinary rank and file. Unless you take that into consideration, then you just become unstuck.'

Feeley remembers looking across the Ebro 'and seeing the bombs and smoke blot out the sun. Nothing could survive, you'd think. Yet when it happened to us and we were bombed in the same way, the only casualties were five mules which had been tied to a tree.

'I remember quite a few of the fellows tied a piece of string around their necks with a piece of wood on it so they could bite on it. The planes came over us so low that you could actually see the bombs coming out. We'd no real anti-aircraft equipment, only machine guns. You'd not a lot of time to duck for cover.

'I remember once looking up and seeing leaflets pouring out like a white cloud. But until you got used to it, being strafed was worse than the bombing.

'Legends grew from nothing during those last days in Spain. One of the people we were told about as a hero was someone called "Peter Martin", and I kept wondering who this brave Peter Martin was. Then on the Ebro front I was taken short in a field and had to answer a call of nature, and the only paper I had in my pocket was an envelope. It had been censored and I saw the censor was the so-called war hero, Peter Martin.

'I only met him once. I was injured – a bullet in the thigh – on the very last day the battalion was in action, 23 September. I couldn't draw my pay for six weeks, and when I finally got it they called out the name of the chap in front and it was Peter Martin . . .'

Eddy Brown, from Glasgow, also got wounded in that last battle. 'I felt something and I rolled back and said to Jock, who I was with, "It's coming from up there, you'd better come back. We're high enough for the enemy to see us." Then I said to him, "I've got wounded, Jock." He says, "Whereabouts?" and I said, "My ankle." He opened my boot and said, "There's bugger-all there. You're no wounded." Then he said, "Oh, Christ, there's blood here," and I'd been wounded in the knee. I'd had a bad ankle since Brunete, and that's where I felt the pain, not in my knee. Then Joe got wounded too.'

The International Brigades paraded in Spain for the last time on 15 November in Barcelona while fighting on the Ebro was still going on. There they were bidden farewell by La Pasionaria and Juan Negrín.

Because of repatriation difficulties, the survivors of the British Battalion did not arrive back in London until 7 December. 'One of my last memories of Spain,' said Bob Cooney, 'was of Barcelona. The air-raid sirens had gone and there was an old lady on her knees praying for God to save her from the Christian general.

'When we got near the frontier the roads were lined with gaunt old men, watching us go. We crossed into France and the French comrades had provided a vast amount of food in the station refreshment room, it was crammed with food. You couldn't believe there was all that hardship just a few miles away.

'Then we got this paper from the British Consul saying that we had to sign it to say we would refund to the government the cost of repatriating us home. I said to the lads, "For Christ's sake sign it. We'll worry about paying for it when we get back . . ."'

On 7 December the 300 British survivors clambered off the train at Victoria Station and supported their wounded up the platform. To their amazement, they found the area outside the station crowded with thousands and thousands of people in a highly emotional state. They were welcomed by Clement Attlee, who said they were the 'heroes of the democratic faith, back once more to continue the struggle in this country'. Other speakers included Stafford Cripps, Willie Gallacher, Tom Mann and Will Lawther, and, in the crowd, was the young Edward Heath.

Sam Wild replied, saying that the battalion intended to keep the promise made to the Spanish people 'that we will change our front but we will continue to fight'.

They raised their banner, and led by three wounded men and to a drum and bugle band the battalion marched together for the last time out of the station and back into the world outside.

Epilogue

'Any man's death diminishes me, because I am involved in mankind' – *John Donne*

It was to take almost forty years for the Franco régime to pass away, and then it was death that took the Caudillo, not force of arms. The year 1977 finally saw General Elections in Spain where the Spanish Socialist Party, headed by Felipe González, made a considerable impact, although the Communist Party did not do so well.

But the situation is fluid, and as Santiago Carrillo, the great communist leader, said at the 1977 Labour Party Conference, democracy in Spain is still very fragile indeed.

The veterans of the International Brigade picked up the threads of their lives. There was no emotional welcome awaiting those who had been prisoners-of-war, but it was unlikely that this mattered to them. Joe Norman says: 'After we were contacted by the Red Cross, things became easier. We began to dare to think we'd see our loved ones again. After six months as a prisoner a representative arrived from the Foreign Office about the exchange of prisoners.

'A month later we went to an Italian camp and had showers and clean shirts. The commandant grew tomatoes and some of us helped ourselves and Bernard McKenna was handcuffed to the wire of the camp from sunrise to sunset after that. The commandant threatened to shoot the next thief. But it was soon over and we went back, through

142

France, to Britain.'

There were no more dole queues as the country finally began to gear itself up for war. Some of the veterans, like Maurice Levine and Sid Quinn, joined up and fought through the Second World War. For the lads from the Glasgow shipyards and the mining valleys of South Wales, work was now no problem as they found themselves in the most essential industries.

Some – Jack Jones, Will Paynter and George Aitken – rose steadily to the top of the trade-union movement. Will Paynter remained a communist until his retirement. George Aitken left the party on the eve of the Second World War over the signing of the Nazi-Soviet Pact and became a leading member of the Labour Party.

Virtually all of them remained politically active, either in the Communist Party or the Labour Party – although the Russian invasion of Hungary in 1956 and of Czechoslovakia in 1968 drove many Communist Party members out.

Fighting in Spain did hamper the careers of several of the men. 'My involvement in Spain was always held against me as a black mark,' says Walter Greenhalgh. 'In the last war I was in personnel selection at the War Office, but I was always noted as an anti-fascist.

'I was restricted to the rank of staff sergeant, although my corporal became a colonel. I feel that many members of the Labour Party, which I joined in 1956, have never trusted me even during the years I served on Brent Council. I suppose after going to Spain I just never suffered fools gladly.'

Sam Wild spent his time at first raising money for the dependants of those killed or wounded in Spain, 'but this came to an end eventually, by which time the war was on'. His tremendous skill and brilliant military reputation availed him nothing. 'They decided I was a bad element. I tried desperately hard to get into either the navy or the army, but they wouldn't have me.

'Then I tried civilian jobs such as civil defence and air-raid warden and so on, but every time I was blocked by the

143

Chief Constable who was in charge of these supposedly anti-Nazi bodies, and he just refused to have me. When I challenged him and said I'd take it to a higher authority, he said he was the highest authority and that he could decide who and who not to take.

'The frustration was terrible. Then, in 1945, I was reading the *Manchester Guardian* and I read that Spanish Republicans were interned in a Chorley mill which had been turned into an internment camp and that one had committed suicide by jumping from a seven-storey window after German and Italian prisoners-of-war had been put in there to await repatriation. I immediately went to the place and demanded to see the authorities and found it was true. I was absolutely embittered and enraged.

'Anyway, I wrote to the Foreign Secretary and the Manchester MPs, and finally, thanks to pressure from all sides, including a fairly progressive Foreign Office, they were eventually released. Some stayed here, but the majority went to France. After Spain, I consider this the best achievement of my adult life.'

Others settled down much as before. Charles Morgan married one of his 29,000 correspondents, 'exchanging one civil war for another, you might say'.

To all the survivors now, Spain still remains the most unique experience. Whatever differences of a political nature may have divided them since, they come together over the war in Spain, 'the Spanish War'.

Sam Wild 'learned about the right kind of discipline in Spain. You looked up to fine people who drew discipline out of you, rather than imposed it on you, because you worked in a common cause. It's something future generations will need to think about. I often think of all those Romans and Greeks and Persians – there was no veneration from the rank and file in those days. In Spain there was a kind of mutuality which became blessed.

'I learned that even when you are in command it is not possible to really know in advance what a battle is going to be like. Even if you are someone like Montgomery in the

Second War, with lots of information, you still couldn't really know what was going to happen. You have to experience actual warfare, and when it arrives you decide in your own simple way what you are going to do about it.

'Spain made me a working-class snob. I've had experiences of all kinds, but the happiest days of my life were spent in Spain. For the first time I recognized the dignity, the goodness and the bravery of ordinary people, in this case the Spanish people. I also experienced the comradeship of my own people – the British – which I had not believed to be possible. I've been through life, joined the navy, been all over the world, and seen the poverty, degradation and exploitation of peoples everywhere, but I've never met people I could appreciate like the Spanish people and the British who went to Spain.'

Says Garry McCartney: 'Of those of us fortunate enough to come back, we would all be of the same mind. The pledge taken by the Brigaders – that only the fronts would change – has been honoured. Those of us who fought for the Republic, not just from Britain but from everywhere, played a tremendous role. Within the trade-union and labour movements we were at least able to give support to the continuing and tremendous fight of the Spanish people with the result that, after forty years, we've just seen the first Spanish General Election since the war. The other memorable aspect was the support of the ordinary British people – they had so much better a grasp of what was happening than the people who were supposed to be leading them.'

Little William Josephs is 'only five foot two but, hen, ever since I got back from Spain when I go in my pub for a drink then I'm *six feet tall*!' Miles tall, another comrade commented of him.

Charles Morgan remembers 'so much, so vividly. I remember an old Spanish peasant telling me, "Carol" – they can't say Charles in Spain, no *ch* – "Carol, I work in the fields from when the sun come from his bed" – they speak so poetic – "I work and when the sun go down and go back to his bed, I go to my wife and my house. I work from dawn until sunset and I get three pesetas a day for six days a week. These are long days." His face was like Clapham Junction with lines and his hands like elephant hide with hard labour, and three pesetas a day was about sevenpence halfpenny in the old money. "I give one peseta to the landlord, one to the church and the other is for my wife and four children," he told me.

'I thought, my God, you were grumbling, Charlie, because you got 15s. 3d. in England on the dole. You lived like a bloody lord compared to these people. They've nothing to lose, they've got to fight to the finish. On 15s. 3d. in England your standard of living was a little bed-sitting room outside Manchester, trips to the pictures, a bowl of soup down the teetotal.

'When I saw the conditions out there, I couldn't believe it. I came back a different person, and I've stayed that way ever since. I've never consciously let down my class from that day to this, and I learned it the hard way – not from textbooks and lectures – but from Spain.'

Bill Feeley 'loved Spain. If the Republic had won I would have lived there. It was a better place to live than Britain in the 'thirties. Their living standard was lower and much of it was very primitive, but if the Republic had won then at least they would have been making progress in the right direction.

'I'd love to have tried it. When you are young you think you have time for anything in the world. When you get to my age you wonder how you are going to cram everything in to the rest of your life. But Spain was different – it was not only the head but the heart that was affected. We were affected emotionally by Spain, and those years in Spain were the finest hours of the British left, of the British labour movement, I saw in my lifetime.

'Yes, it changed me. Any experience changes you, every day of your life – men aren't static. But Spain had an overwhelming influence which is hard to express. It was the biggest event of all our lives, and for me the only significant thing which ever happened to me. We've remained aware, ever since, of the struggles for freedom in the rest of the world, but there was never anything again like Spain.'

Fred Copeman 'got to be a battalion commander from an ordinary soldier, and I did as well as I could so that nobody could point the finger at me and say I didn't try and do things well.

'You can never talk enough about it – hell, we had the finest, bravest men in the world out there. We had the ordinary workers, the scientists, the poets and the writers, and in Spain they were truly equal to one another.'

'It was the most important thing I did,' says Bob Doyle. 'It taught me what is important in this life is a democratically elected socialist government, and that you have to be prepared to fight, if necessary, to keep it. If they had stopped Franco I don't believe the last war would have been necessary – of course, I'm glad I went.'

'We had a fine cross-section of the British working class in Spain,' says George Aitken, 'and some fine middle class too, but the working class were the backbone. Even if there was a handful of scroungers and people who wished they'd never seen Spain, most of them were the finest people you could possibly imagine. They would fight on irrespective of anything.

'Obviously it was one of the great experiences of my life. Spain was something the like of which you can't imagine today. I'll always remember the homecoming of the battalion. When they got to Victoria it was absolutely unbelievable, the great square outside was chock-a-block with people, absolutely crammed. The Labour Party leaders were there – even Ted Heath, who'd visited Spain with a student delegation, was tnere with some Tories.

'It made me feel as if the Spanish people had their arms pinioned while the fascists beat them and hit them in the face – and it was we who were standing and holding their arms.'

For Maurice Levine: 'It made the most tremendous impact on me and influenced me ever after, especially in my way of thinking. I know people who've done very well financially after being a rebel or a red in the 'thirties, but it's never appealed to me since I felt the feeling of fascism in the air in those days.

'I feel so proud to have gone to Spain, proud to have been a part of it and of the comradeship that there was between us. I served in the last war, too, from the Normandy beaches to Hamburg, but it was a different kind of thing altogether.

'In Spain you were so terribly ill-equipped against your opponents and the masses of stuff they threw at you, but you also felt you were on the right side, fighting for something right and proper. It was the last crusade. It could never happen in the world as it is today. At least you were a little part of the history of that period, which was very important.'

'It was the event of a lifetime, the highspot of my life,' says Bob Cooney. 'I have a great love for the Spanish people and great hope for their future. Freedom is infectious. So we went to Spain so we could defeat Hitler. Those who went to fight in Spain were the apprentices of freedom who became freedom's craftsmen.'

'Spain,' says Walter Greenhalgh, 'was not like the Grunwick picket line – you couldn't join the battle in the morning and then go home and watch yourself on the telly before settling down for supper and bed.

'With very few exceptions, it was accepted that once you were there you were involved completely – for better or worse.

'It didn't take long for us to have doubts, disillusion, frustration, and very often the fervent wish to be anywhere except where we were at the moment. Nevertheless I have never doubted – nor have I come across any of my comrades who doubted – that serving with the International Brigade was the most worthwhile and significant period of my life. One lasting result has been to give me a pride in my working-class origins that nothing and nobody since has ever been able to shake.'

For Will Paynter: 'The men of the British Battalion were

heroes who fought and suffered for a just cause, and nothing can be said or written to take that glory away from them – and the same can be said of the nurses, doctors, first-aid men and ambulance drivers who worked so tirelessly to help the sick and wounded.'

Sid Quinn is happy, at least, that he has lived to see 'the beginnings of democracy again in Spain. It had to come, but this time our Spanish comrades did not want a bloodbath. I want to go back there and walk down those little village streets and see the Spanish people again and pay my respects to all those fine, wee fellows who were killed there. Although I experienced the Second World War, it was not the same.

'The world stopped for us in 1939.'

Select Bibliography

Blaye, Édouard de, *Franco and the Politics of Spain*, Penguin Books, Harmondsworth, 1976.

Book of the XVth Brigade, The, edited by Frank Ryan, War Commissariat, Madrid, 1938.

Borkenau, Frank, *The Spanish Cockpit*, Faber & Faber, London, 1937.

Brenan, Gerald, *The Spanish Labyrinth*, Cambridge University Press, 1943.

Carrillo, Santiago, *Eurocommunism and the State*, Lawrence & Wishart, London, 1977.

Francis, Hywel, 'Welsh Miners and the Spanish Civil War', *Journal of Contemporary History*, vol. 5, No. 3, 1970.

Gurney, Jason, *Crusade in Spain*, Faber & Faber, London, 1974.

Orwell, George, *Homage to Catalonia*, Secker & Warburg, London, 1938.

Paynter, Will, *My Generation*, Allen & Unwin, London, 1972.

Rust, William, *Britons in Spain*, Lawrence & Wishart, London, 1938.

Stansky, Peter, and William Abrahams, *Journey to the Frontier*, Constable, London, 1966.

Thomas, Hugh, *The Spanish Civil War*, Eyre & Spottiswoode, London, 1961; revised edition, Penguin Books, Harmondsworth, 1976.